# MEDIAEVAL SOURCES
IN TRANSLATION

## 28

Ibn Sīnā

# REMARKS AND ADMONITIONS
# PART ONE: LOGIC

Translated from the original Arabic
with an Introduction and Notes

by

SHAMS CONSTANTINE INATI

PONTIFICAL INSTITUTE OF MEDIAEVAL STUDIES

ACKNOWLEDGMENT

Publication of this book was assisted
by a grant from the
National Endowment for the Humanities.

CANADIAN CATALOGUING IN PUBLICATION DATA

Avicenna, 980-1037.
  [Ishārāt wa-al-tanbīhāt. English]
  Remarks and admonitions : part one : logic

(Mediaeval sources in translation, ISSN 0316-0874 ; 28)
Bibliography: p.
ISBN 0-88844-277-7

1. Logic - Early works to 1800.   I. Inati, Shams Constantine,
1945-   II. Pontifical Institute of Mediaeval Studies.   III. Title.
IV. Title: Ishārāt wa-al-tanbīhāt. English.   V. Series.

B751.I62E6 1984           160           C83-098888-2

© 1984 by

Pontifical Institute of Mediaeval Studies
59 Queen's Park Crescent East
Toronto, Ontario, Canada M5S 2C4

PRINTED BY UNIVERSA PRESS, WETTEREN, BELGIUM

*To the memory of my brother,
Doctor Yakub Inati,
who guided me from childhood,
both intellectually and emotionally.*

# Contents

Acknowledgments .................................... XIII

Abbreviations ...................................... XIV

Introduction ....................................... 1
  I. A General Word .............................. 1
  II. Analysis of the Text ........................ 5
  — 1. Conception and Assent 5. — 2. Function and Use of Logic 6. — 3. Logic as a Branch of Philosophy or Only as a Tool of It 9. — 4. Preliminary Notes 11. — 5. Single Expressions 13. — 6. The Explanatory Phrase 19. — 7. On Propositions 21. — 8. The Proof 34. — 9. On Demonstration 38.
  III. A Word About the Translation ............... 43

### Remarks and Admontions, Part One: Logic

The First Method: Concerning the Purpose of Logic ....... 47
  1. Remark: [Concerning the knowledge of the composite as requiring knowledge of single elements] ....... 48
  2. Remark: [Concerning the logician's need for taking into consideration universal language] .......... 48
  3. Remark: [Concerning conception and assent] ..... 49
  4. Remark: [Concerning the logician's need for knowing the principles of the explanatory phrase and proof] 50
  5. Remark: Concerning the expression as a sign for the concept ......................................... 50
  6. Remark: Concerning the predicate .............. 51
  7. Remark: Concerning single and composite expressions ......................................... 51

| | |
|---|---|
| 8. Remark: Concerning individual and universal expressions | 52 |
| 9. Remark: Concerning the essential, the concomitant accidental, and the separable accidental | 53 |
| 10. Remark: Concerning the constitutive essential | 54 |
| 11. Remark: Concerning the non-constitutive concomitant accidental | 55 |
| 12. Remark: Concerning the non-concomitant accidental | 57 |
| 13. Remark: [Concerning the accidental] | 57 |
| 14. Remark: Concerning the essential in another sense | 57 |
| 15. Remark: Concerning that which is stated as the answer to the question, "What is it?" | 58 |
| 16. Remark: Concerning the various types of that which is stated as the answer to the question, "What is it?" | 60 |
| The Second Method: On the Five Simple Terms, the Definition and the Description | 64 |
| 1. Remark: Concerning that which is stated as the answer to the question, "What is it?" as "genus"; and that which is stated as the answer to the question, "What is it?" as "species" | 64 |
| 2. Remark: Concerning the arrangement of genus and species | 65 |
| 3. Remark: Concerning the difference | 65 |
| 4. Remark: Concerning property and the common accident | 67 |
| 5. Admonition | 69 |
| 6. Remark: Concerning the description of the five [terms] | 69 |
| 7. Remark: Concerning definition | 70 |
| 8. Delusion and Admonition | 71 |
| 9. Remark: Concerning description | 72 |
| 10. Remark: Concerning the types of errors that occur in the identification of things by definition and description | 73 |
| 11. Delusion and Admonition | 75 |
| The Third Method: On Assertive Composition | 77 |
| 1. Remark: Concerning the types of propositions | 77 |
| 2. Remark: Concerning affirmation and negation | 78 |

3. Remark: Concerning singularity, indefiniteness and definiteness .............................. 80
4. Remark: Concerning the judgment of the indefinite proposition ................................ 81
5. Remark: Concerning the definiteness and indefiniteness of conditional propositions ............... 82
6. Remark: Concerning the composition of conditional propositions from predicative ones ............. 83
7. Remark: Concerning equipollence and positiveness  83
8. Remark: Concerning conditional propositions ..... 86
9. Remark: Concerning the dispositions that accompany propositions, and that give them specific judgments in definiteness and in other cases ................. 88
10. Remark: Concerning the conditions of propositions  89

The Fourth Method: The Matters and Modes of Propositions  90

1. Remark: Concerning the matters of propositions .. 90
2. Remark: Concerning the modes of propositions, and the difference between an absolute and a necessary proposition ................................. 91
3. Remark: Concerning the mode of possibility ...... 95
4. Remark: Concerning principles and conditions for the modes ...................................... 97
5. Remark: Concerning the determination of the universal affirmative in the modes ................... 99
6. Remark: Concerning the determination of the universal negative in the modes .................... 101
7. Admonition: Concerning points of disagreement and agreement between the consideration of the mode and that of predication .......................... 102
8. Remark: Concerning the determination of the two particular propositions and the modes ........... 103
9. Remark: Concerning the implication of modal propositions ....................................... 104
10. Delusion and Admonition .................... 105

The Fifth Method: On the Contradiction and Conversion of Propositions ................................. 107

A general word concerning contradiction .......... 107

1. Remark: Concerning the contradiction between absolute propositions, and the determination of the contradictory of absolute and concrete propositions  109
2. Remark: Concerning contradiction in the remaining modal propositions  112
3. Remark: Concerning the conversion of absolute propositions  113
4. Remark: Concerning the conversion of necessary propositions  115
5. Remark: Concerning the conversion of possible propositions  116

The Sixth Method  118
1. Remark: Concerning propositions, with respect to those of them involving assent, and similar ones  118
2. A follow-up  128

The Seventh Method: On Beginning the Second Composition of Proof  129
1. Remark: Concerning the syllogism, induction and analogy  129
2. Remark: Concerning specifically the syllogism  131
3. Remark: Concerning specifically the conjunctive syllogism  133
4. Remark: Concerning the various types of predicative conjunctive syllogisms  134
5. The first figure  135
6. Remark: Concerning the second figure  137
7. Remark: Concerning the third figure  141

The Eighth Method: On Conditional Syllogisms, and on What Follows the Syllogism  144
1. Remark: Concerning conditional conjunctive syllogisms  144
2. Remark: Concerning the syllogism of equals  145
3. Remark: Concerning repetitive conditional syllogisms  145
4. Remark: Concerning the syllogism by contradiction  147

The Ninth Method: In Which a Brief Explication of the
    Demonstrative Science in Given ............... 148
  1. Remark: Concerning the various types of syllogisms,
     with respect to their matters and their production of
     assent .................................... 148
  2. Remark: Concerning the syllogisms and the demonstrative inquiries ......................... 150
  3. Remark: Concerning the subjects, principles, questions [and transference of demonstrations] in the
     sciences .................................. 152
  4. Remark: Concerning the correspondence of the
     sciences .................................. 153
  5. Remark: Concerning causal demonstration and factual demonstration ........................ 154
  6. Remark: Concerning the questions [in the sciences] 155

The Tenth Method: On Fallacious Syllogisms ............ 158

Bibliography ....................................... 161

Index .............................................. 163

# Acknowledgments

I would like to express my appreciation to Professor George Hourani, Department of Philosophy, SUNY at Buffalo, and to Professor Michael Marmura, Department of Middle East and Islamic Studies, University of Toronto, for their insightful and constructive comments. I would also like to acknowledge the State University of New York at Buffalo for providing necessary facilities, and a stimulating and friendly atmosphere.

I would like to extend my special gratitude to my family and friends for their emotional support and encouragement throughout this project. I also wish to thank my assistant, James Mack, for being highly responsible and patient, and for his care in typing and proofreading the manuscript.

The preparation of this volume was made possible in part by a grant from the Translations Program of the National Endowment for the Humanities.

S. C. I.

# Abbreviations

*Anal. Post.*   Aristotle, *Analytica Posteriora*
*Anal. Pr.*   Aristotle, *Analytica Priora*
*Tr. Log.*   Ibn Sīnā, *Avicenna's Treatise on Logic*, ed. Zabeeh.
*Sh. Com.*   al-Farābī, *Short Commentary on Aristotle's Prior Analytics*, trans. Rescher.
*De Int.*   Aristotle, *De Interpretatione*
*Ish.*   Ibn Sīnā, *al-Ishārāt wat-Tanbīhāt*
*Dir. Rem.*   Ibn Sīnā, *Livre des directives et remarques*, trans. Goichon.
*Man.*   Ibn Sīnā, *Manṭiq al-Mashriqiyyīn*
*Meta.*   Aristotle, *Metaphysica*
*Naj.*   Ibn Sīnā, *an-Najāt*
*Prop. Log.*   Ibn Sīnā, *The Propositional Logic of Avicenna*, trans. Shehaby.
*Qas. Muz.*   Ibn Sīnā, *al-Qaṣīda al-Muzdawija*
*Sh. Bur.*   Ibn Sīnā, *ash-Shifā', al-Manṭiq, al-Burhān*, ed. Afifi.
*Sh. Mad.*   Ibn Sīnā, *ash-Shifā', al-Manṭiq, al-Madkhal*, ed. Madkour et al.
*Sh. Q.*   Ibn Sīnā, *ash-Shifā', al-Manṭiq, al-Qiyās*, ed. Zayed.

*Note*: All references to the text of *al-Ishārāt wat-Tanbīhāt* are to the pages of Dunyā's edition, as found in the margin of this translation.

# Introduction

## I. A GENERAL WORD

This book on logic is the first of a four-part work, *al-Ishārāt wat-Tanbīhāt* (*Remarks and Admonitions*)[1] by Ibn Sīnā.[2] The other three parts[3] are, in order, *Physics*, *Metaphysics* and *Sufism*. Why the work begins with logic will become clear in our analysis of the text.

The exact date for Ibn Sīnā's writing of *al-Ishārāt wat-Tanbīhāt* is not known. However, it is known to be a late work. It can, therefore, be taken to represent the author's mature ideas and firm convictions.

The work consists mainly of brief presentations of Ibn Sīnā's views, as well as attacks on some of his predecessors and contemporaries. The sections including the former are titled "Remarks," and the sections including the latter are on the whole titled "Admonitions";[4] thus, the whole work came to be called *Remarks and Admonitions*.

The reasons that have led us to embark on translating and annotating this work are first that it will open for the English reader, who does not command the language of the original text, the opportunity to examine for himself, among other things, the views which were the subject of great controversies in medieval Islam – not as they were presented in books of philosophers with diverging views that have already been translated into English, such as al-Ghazali's

---

[1] Our translation of this text is based on Sulaymān Dunyā's second edition (Cairo: Dar al-Ma'ārif fī Maṣr, 1971). But this edition was often compared to that of Jacques Forget (Leiden, 1892); and with that of Nabil Shehaby (Tehran, 1960).

[2] Ibn Sīnā, known to the West as Avicenna, lived from 980-1037 A.D. For further information on his life, see William E. Gohlman, *The Life of Ibn Sīnā* (Albany: SUNY Press, 1974).

[3] A translation of these parts is now being prepared.

[4] In some places these sections are also called "Delusions," or "Delusions and Admonitions." It must also be mentioned that some sections of this work are given different titles, such as "A Follow-Up"; but these sections are few in number.

*The Incoherence of Philosophers* and Ibn Rushd's *The Incoherence of Incoherence*, but as they were presented by their own author.

Second, a translation of this work makes available to the reader the most concise and comprehensive account on Ibn Sīnā's late philosophical system. This will be useful not only for familiarizing the reader with Ibn Sīnā's ideas, but will also shed some light on the views of those who influenced him, such as Aristotle and the Stoics, and those who were influenced by him, such as St. Thomas Aquinas.

It must be mentioned that this is the first translation of this work into English, and the first translation of a whole philosophical work of Ibn Sīnā from Arabic into English. There is a French translation by A. M. Goichon under the title *Livre des directives et remarques*.[5] However even though this French translation was an important step toward understanding *al-Ishārāt wat-Tanbīhāt*, it, nevertheless, distorts its contents at many points (compare, for example, that work with our translation of the First Method, Chapter 7 and the Third Method, Chapter 8). An example of the most misleading translation is that of the following passage: "thus repeating [a part] of it yields only the contradictory of the rest."[6] Here is Goichon's rendering of the passage: "... [tel est le cas] lorsque le choix de l'œil est le seul à amener une conclusion, et celle-ci est le contraire du conséquent, uniquement."[7]

Third, in this translation there is also a benefit for the Arabic-speaking reader whether a layman or a scholar. As we will see, the Arabic text is written in a highly difficult style. Its statements are concise and many of its sentences are elliptical. Much clarification and much explanation is needed before the reader can grasp its ideas. We hope that our translation is careful and clear enough that together with the introduction and notes it will aid the reader in assimilating the text.

Our fourth main reason for undertaking this work was that the task appeared as a great personal challenge. The work is a collection of notes about a large number of principles, many of which are difficult to understand. Little elaboration or explanation is given. The

---

[5] A. M. Goichon, *Livre des directives et remarques* (Paris: Librairie Philosophique, J. Vrin, 1948).

[6] *Ish.*, Part I, pp. 451-452.

[7] Goichon, *Dir. Rem.*, p. 220. For the Arabic text, see Eighth Method, note 9.

work is also difficult in other respects: as mentioned, many of its sentences are incomplete; some sentences are interrupted by parts of earlier or later sentences; and the punctuation is, on the whole, inappropriate. All of this has left the work much like a collection of riddles to which we, wondering whether we were up to the task, applied every available method to solve.

Whether or not all these difficulties were intended by the author is not clear; after all, Ibn Sīnā is not known for a clear and elegant style. What is clear though is that the work was intended to be highly difficult in order to prevent its accessibility to the majority of readers. The closing section of the fourth part indicates this. Addressing his select reader, Ibn Sīnā says: "Protect this truth from the ignorant, the vulgar, those who are not endowed with the sharpness of mind, the skill and habit, those who lend an ear to the crowds, those who have gone astray from philosophy and have fallen behind." [8] And according to Ibn Sīnā, such is the majority of people. Ibn Sīnā did not wish any except the elite to be able to have access to the contents of *al-Ishārāt wat-Tanbīhāt* – the elite being those endowed with high intelligence, goodness of heart, honesty of mind and love for philosophy and appreciation of its value. In other words, the elite are those that Ibn Sīnā classifies in *Manṭiq al-Mashriqiyyīn* as "ourselves and those who are like ourselves." [9] Ibn Sīnā is confident that intelligent readers are capable of grasping the hidden truths of the work, as well as supplying the relevant details:

> For you, who are anxious to determine the truth, I have prepared in these *Remarks and Admonitions* principles and generalities of wisdom. If you are directed by intelligence, it would be easy for you to subdivide them and work out the specific details.[10]

But why should Ibn Sīnā deprive those readers who are as unlucky as not to be of the elite from having access to this work? Why not present its ideas in such a form as to make them readily understood by such readers? It is because, according to him, there is no way to

---

[8] *Ish.*, Part IV, Dār al-Maʿārif fī Maṣr (Cairo, 1958), pp. 904-906.
[9] Ibn Sīnā, *Manṭiq al-Mashriqiyyīn* (Cairo: Salafiyya Press, 1328 A.H.), p. 4.
[10] *Ish.*, Part I, p. 114.

make such readers understand such profound truths. If you were to try to make them understand them, you would be trying in vain since such readers lack the proper instrument for grasping these truths. And since they cannot grasp them, they will end up misunderstanding and distorting them. The best thing then is to hide these truths from such readers. Ibn Sīnā goes as far as to plead with the elite not to try to communicate the ideas of *al-Ishārāt wat-Tanbīhāt* to the commoners, but only to those who are pure of heart, with good conduct and willing to consider the hasty doubts that they may have; and even to those, the truths must be communicated gradually, with apprehension and with a request that they do the same in protecting these truths.[11]

The best method for dealing with the difficulties that arose in the course of the work proved to be a constant checking of Ibn Sīnā's views in his other writings. The following works of Ibn Sīnā were most helpful in understanding this first part: *ash-Shifā', al-Manṭiq, al-Madkhal (Healing, Logic, Isagoge)*;[12] *ash-Shifā', al-Manṭiq, al-Qiyās (Healing, Logic, On the Syllogism)*;[13] *ash-Shifā', al-Manṭiq, al-Burhān (Healing, Logic, On Demonstration)*;[14] *an-Najāt, al-Manṭiq (Deliverance, Logic)*;[15] *Manṭiq al-Mashriqiyyin (Logic of Orientals)*. Also the following works were occasionally consulted: aṭ-Ṭūsī, *Commentary*;[16] and Zabeeh, *Avicenna's Treatise on Logic*.[17]

---

[11] *Ish.*, Part IV, pp. 904-906.

[12] Ibn Sīnā, *ash-Shifā', al-Manṭiq, al-Madkhal*, eds. G. Anawātī, M. al-Khuḍairī and F. al-Ahwānī, revised by I. Madkour (Cairo: al-Maṭba'a al-Amīriyya, 1952).

[13] *ash-Shifā', al-Manṭiq, al-Qiyās*, ed. S. Zayed (Cairo, 1964).

[14] Ibn Sīnā, *ash-Shifā', al-Manṭiq, al-Burhān*, ed. A. E. Afīfī, revised by I. Madkour (Cairo, 1956).

[15] Ibn Sīnā, *an-Najāt*, ed. M. S. al-Kurdī (Cairo, 1938).

[16] Naṣīr ad-Dīn aṭ-Ṭūsī, *Commentary*, published with *Ish.*, in the same edition of *Ish.* that we are using. This is not a commentary on *Ish.* only, but also a commentary on Fakhr ad-Dīn ar-Rāzī's commentary on *Ish.*, *Lubāb al-Ishārāt*. In *Lubāb al-Ishārāt*, ar-Rāzī not only elaborates Ibn Sīnā's views, but also attempts a refutation of a number of them. It is for this reason that his commentary was dubbed "pejorative" (*jarḥan*) (aṭ-Ṭūsī, *Commentary*, p. 112). Aṭ-Ṭūsī's commentary, on *Ish.* on the other hand, is a sympathetic interpretation.

[17] Ibn Sīnā, *Avicenna's Treatise on Logic*, translated by F. Zabeeh (The Hague: Martinus Nijhoff, 1971).

## II. ANALYSIS OF THE TEXT

Our purpose now is to give a clear outline of the major ideas in the first part of *al-Ishārāt wat-Tanbīhāt*. No defense or refutation of any of these ideas will be given. Neither time nor space permits that. So let us attempt a brief exposition of Ibn Sīnā's views in the simplest language possible. For this purpose we will draw upon much material from his other works, in order to understand and pull together his logical system.

We wish to mention that, even though we feel that most of the difficulties of the work have been delineated, there remain some for which we have not found solutions – these are specifically some of the sources referred to by Ibn Sīnā.

### 1. CONCEPTION AND ASSENT

Ibn Sīnā emphasizes that knowledge is of two types: *taṣawwur* (conception, picturing, form-grasping, imaging) and *taṣdīq* (declarative phrase,[18] i.e., true or false; a relation in the mind, of correspondence between the concept and the thing for which the concept stands,[19] i.e., truth;[20] assent that the relation of correspondence between the concept and the nature it represents is true[21] – it is in this last sense that we will be using the term as Ibn Sīnā seems to be doing for the most part).

Conception is the grasping of an object without any kind of judgment – it is this grasped object which we call "concept." Concepts are either simple, single or composite. A simple concept is

---

[18] *al-Qaṣīda al-Muzdawija* in *Man.*, p. 17.

[19] *Sh. Mad.*, p. 17.

[20] This statement in *Sh. Mad.* is misleading. It is clear in *Man.* (p. 60) that this relation of correspondence is called *ṣādiqan* (true), while *taṣdīq* is said to be the belief that this relation is true (ibid.).

[21] Ibid. This is to be distinguished from falsification, rejection or denial of the correspondence of such a relation (*takdhīb*). Every assent is an acceptance and an assertion; but what it accepts could be an affirmation or a negation. "I accept that A is B," or "I accept that A is not B" are both assents. Further, according to Ibn Sīnā, assents can be either true or false (this will become clear later on in this introduction in our discussion of propositions involving assent). But this, of course, raises the question as to whether assent is worthy of being called a form of knowledge, as our philosopher thinks.

one in which there are no parts, such as the concept "God" – "God", according to Ibn Sīnā, is a concept that represents a simple nature. A single concept is one which may or may not have parts, but were it to have parts, these parts could not stand alone as long as they are parts of this concept. A simple concept is a single one, but the converse is not true. Examples of a single concept are: "human being," "triangle" and "angel." Finally, a composite concept is one in which there is at least one single concept as a part of it. This is exemplified by the concept "mortal rational animal," "shall we walk?"[22] and "do this."[23] It must be mentioned that the above examples of the various types of concepts are given by Ibn Sīnā as examples of objects of conception, without specification as to which of them exemplify which kind of concepts. The specification is ours. Since the classification of concepts we have just given is that of Ibn Sīnā (though never made clear in *al-Ishārāt wat-Tanbīhāt*),[24] we thought it would be more helpful to divide the examples in accordance with the division of concepts, rather than lump them under "objects of conception."

Assent is the grasping of an object, but it differs from conception in that it is always accompanied by a judgment (of the type specified above). Assent presupposes conception. The reason is that if someone says, "Every white is an accident," you either believe this or you do not. But whether you believe it or whether you doubt it, you must first be able to conceive and understand what is meant by it. But while every assent presupposes conception, the converse is not true.[25] For you can conceive and understand something without making any judgment about it.

2. FUNCTION AND USE OF LOGIC

Objects of conception divide into two kinds: (1) that which is known and (2) that which is unknown.[26] The same is true of the

---

[22] *Man.*, p. 9.

[23] *Sh. Mad.*, p. 17.

[24] Except perhaps in an indirect manner: through an analysis of expressions which are said first, to correspond to concepts; and second, to divide into simple expressions, single expressions and composite or compound expressions.

[25] *Sh. Mad.*, p. 17.

[26] If the object of conception is one which is already grasped by the mind, i.e.,

objects of assent. We have (1) that which is known and (2) that which is unknown. The objects known by conception and those known by assent are, of course, not objects of inquiry; while those not so known are. But what is known and what is unknown is relative to the mind of a certain individual. However, some objects of conception are known to every normal mind. These are the self-evident concepts: the objects that present themselves to the mind immediately. "Being," "thing" and "necessary" are, according to Ibn Sīnā, examples of such concepts.[27] Leaving these very few immediate objects of conception aside, the rest of the objects of conception divide, with respect to the mind of an individual, into what has been already acquired (known by mediation: either of self-evident concepts or others that have been already acquired), and what has not yet been acquired (the unknown object of conception). Which objects have already been acquired by the mind and which have not, is, of course, a relative matter. Thus when Ibn Sīnā gives us "human being" or "triangle" as examples of known concepts, the question is "known to whom?" It seems Ibn Sīnā is saying that such objects are acquired by the normal adult human being. Objects such as "binomial" or "disconnected" are, on the other hand, not acquired by such a person, but require consideration and inquiry.

Also some objects of assent are known by the human mind immediately, without the mediation of other assents, such as "two is the half of four" or "the whole is greater than the part." Other objects of assent are acquired, such as "the world is a composite." And finally, to some minds, there are objects that are not yet grasped by assent, such as that the square on the diagonal is equal to the squares of the sides of the right angle which it subtends.

According to Ibn Sīnā, a human being should acquire as much knowledge as possible. For it is by knowledge and knowledge alone

---

known, the question arises as to how can one speak of unknown object of conception? An unknown object of conception is one which the mind has the capacity to grasp; however, it is not yet grasped. In other words, it is known potentially, but unknown actually.

[27] *ash-Shifā', al-Ilāhiyyāt*, eds. G. Anawātī, S. Dunyā and S. Zāyed, revised and introduced by I. Madkour (Cairo, 1960), pp. 29, 292.

that human happiness can be achieved. Two forms of knowledge are required for this: practical knowledge and theoretical knowledge. The former is knowledge of what must be done for the perfection of society, the family and the individual. Practical knowledge prepares the way for theoretical knowledge by means of which the metaphysical perfection of the individual is completed.[28] The metaphysical perfection of the individual is completed by knowledge of the essences, natures, realities or quiddities[29] of things, which are the eternal elements of this universe. How one can grasp these essences will become clear later on. Meanwhile, it must be said that knowledge of essences serves to perfect an individual by making him mirror the eternal aspect of the universe, and hence achieve eternity for himself – eternity being identified with happiness.

For the purpose of increasing our happiness we must, therefore, reduce the amount of unknown objects of conception and unknown objects of assent. To do this, there is only one way: to get from a known object of conception to an unknown one and from a known object of assent to an unknown one. The means of getting from a known object of conception to an unknown one is called "explanatory phrase."[30] And the means of getting from a known object of assent to an unknown one is called "proof." Thus if you do not know what "human being" is, the way to acquire knowledge of it is through a phrase that explains to you what it is, such as "human being is a rational animal." But the simple elements[31] of which this phrase consists, i.e., "rational" and "animal" must be known concepts. If, for example, you do not know what "rational" is, you

---

[28] For a discussion of how practical knowledge prepares the way for theoretical knowledge, see my Ph.D. dissertation, "*An Examination of Ibn Sīnā's Solution for the Problem of Evil*," Chapter Four (SUNY at Buffalo, 1979).

[29] "Essence" (*thāt*), "nature" (*ṭabīa*), "reality" (*ḥaqīqa*), and "quiddity" (*māhiyya*) are used interchangeably by Ibn Sīnā.

[30] In *Ish.*, the only method mentioned for getting from the known concept to the unknown one is the explanatory phrase. In *Sh. Mad.* (p. 18), other methods are mentioned: name, example and sign. In the latter work, he says that it is not customary to give a common name to these various types of phrases; or if it is customary, this common name has not reached him (ibid.).

[31] By "simple element" is meant the single unit of a phrase (*Sh. Mad.*, p. 21), i.e., the single concept, whether simple, in an absolute sense, or having parts. Thus when "simple" is made an attribute of "element" or "part" or a phrase, it is used in a relative sense, i.e., simple in relation to the whole.

could not know what "human being" is. That is why, in an unknown object of conception, we must first start from known concepts that are put together in a phrase that explains the unknown object of conception. The same is true of assents. One has to start with known assents which, then, are put together in order to lead to knowledge of an unknown object of assent.

But of explanatory phrases and proofs there are those that are valid (real) and which lead to the certain knowledge sought, and those that are invalid (unreal), but resemble the valid, or appear to resemble the valid, and which lead to falsehoods.

Logic is a set of rules that helps one distinguish the valid from the invalid explanatory phrase and proof; and thus it is said to be an instrument for the various branches of knowledge. In short, the function of logic is to help us move from the known to the unknown; and hence help us increase the degree of our knowledge, which in turn elevates the degree of our happiness, the best goal that we can hope to achieve. It is in helping us achieve this goal that the benefit of logic lies.

Ibn Sīnā draws an analogy between logic as a set of rules for scientific thought on the one hand, and grammar and meter as sets of rules for discourse and poetry respectively. But he also sees an important difference: a good, natural mind (*al-fiṭra*) and a good taste, he tells us, could replace respectively the acquisition of grammar and meter, but no natural mind can function in place of logic except if one is guided by God.[32] If the natural mind were sufficient for differentiating the real from the unreal explanatory phrases and proofs, there would not have been any disagreement among thinkers, nor could one have contradicted oneself.[33]

After pointing out the purpose of logic, Ibn Sīnā devotes the rest of this first part to a study of the two methods by means of which logic achieves its purpose, i.e., the explanatory phrase and the proof.

## 3. LOGIC AS A BRANCH OF PHILOSOPHY OR ONLY AS A TOOL OF IT

Before we move on to a study of the explanatory phrase and the proof, a word must be said about Ibn Sīnā's position regarding the question as to whether logic is a part of philosophy or only its tool, a

---

[32] *Sh. Mad.*, p. 19; *Naj.*, p. 5.
[33] *Naj.*, p. 3.

question which had preoccupied the ancient philosophical schools and was still the center of hot debates in Ibn Sīnā's time. The Platonists, for example, considered logic both as a branch of philosophy and as a tool of it. The Peripatetics held that logic is only a tool of philosophy. And the Stoics considered logic a part of philosophy.

Ibn Sīnā does not address this issue in *al-Ishārāt wat-Tanbīhāt*, but he does in *al-Madkhal*. However, since in *al-Ishārāt wat-Tanbīhāt* logic is at some point spoken of as a tool[34] and at another point as a science (philosophy or knowledge),[35] we thought it fit to interject at this point Ibn Sīnā's view on this matter, which will help the reader understand Ibn Sīnā's comfort with speaking of logic both as a tool and as a science.

In preparation for responding to this issue, Ibn Sīnā tells us that essences or natures of things either exist externally, or exist in the mind, or are free from either mode of existence. Accidents and states attach to the natures as they exist either externally or in the mind. The mental accidents and states are exemplified in being subject or predicate, universality or particularity of predication, essentiality or accidentality of predication.[36] Logic treats of nothing except the natures inasmuch as accidents and states attach to them in the mind; and has nothing to do with the natures as they exist either externally, mentally, or as they are free from both modes of existence.[37] This is so because logic is a movement from the known to the unknown, and as such, for one thing, it cannot be concerned with anything outside the mind, since what is known or unknown is such only in relation to a mind;[38] and for another, this movement cannot be carried out except by means of the mental states, as will be seen later.

If philosophy is limited to a study of the natures as they exist both externally and mentally, then logic is not a part of philosophy, but inasmuch as it is helpful for this study, it is a tool of philosophy. If, on the other hand, philosophy encompasses every theoretical study, then logic is a part of philosophy and a tool of its other parts.[39]

---

[34] *Ish.*, Part I, p. 117.
[35] Ibid., p. 127.
[36] *Sh. Mad.*, pp. 15, 22.
[37] Ibid.
[38] Ibid., p. 15.
[39] Ibid., pp. 15-16.

According to Ibn Sīnā, this whole issue proves to be spurious. After all, there is no contradiction between the two views; for in each "philosophy" is taken in a sense different from that taken in the other. Let everyone specify the sense in which one is using "philosophy" and the whole issue will disappear. Besides, concerning oneself with such questions is a futile effort and results in no benefit.[40]

## 4. Preliminary Notes

Both the explanatory phrase and the proof are composed of concepts (which are their matter). And the composition takes a certain form by means of which the concepts are arranged. Ibn Sīnā draws an analogy between the concepts and the composition of the explanatory phrase and the proof, on the one hand, and the matter of a house or a chair and the form of that house or that chair. As we cannot build a house or a chair from just any matter, and in just any form, so also we cannot have an explanatory phrase or a proof from just any concepts, put together in just any manner.[41]

For understanding the explanatory phrase and the proof, it is not important that we understand the concepts in themselves, but only inasmuch as they can be employed as the matter of the explanatory phrase and the proof, inasmuch as they have certain states and relations to each other. When a builder considers wood as the material out of which he wishes to build a house, he does not consider the nature of wood in itself – that is, inasmuch as it has a plant soul, or inasmuch as it is hot or cold by nature, etc. – but only inasmuch as it has certain states due to which it can be used in building the house, such as the fact that it is hard or soft.[42] The same is true of a logician. As has been already mentioned, he must not concern himself with the natures of things as they exist, either externally or in the mind, nor with the natures of things in themselves, i.e., as separate from any mode of existence. Rather, his concern must be these natures inasmuch as they are subjects or predicates, universal or particular, essential or accidental, etc.; in other words, inasmuch as any accident attaches to them as they exist in the mind. It is, therefore, these concepts, taken under the above-mentioned aspect, that are the subject of logic.

[40] Ibid., p. 16.
[41] *Naj.*, pp. 3-4.
[42] *Sh. Mad.*, p. 22.

But concepts which represent in the imagination or the intellect the natures of things[43] are, in turn, represented by language.[44] As it is impossible to understand the natures of things apart from the concepts that correspond to them, so also is it impossible to understand concepts apart from the expressions that stand for them. Thus even though the ultimate goal of a human being is the understanding of the natures of things, and the ultimate goal of the logician is the understanding of concepts, taken under the previously-mentioned aspect, the former must make it his purpose to precede his goal by the study of concepts; and the latter must make it his purpose to precede his goal by the study of expressions.

We are reminded, though, that the subject of logic is not language, but that a study of language is necessitated by the need for discourse and dialogue,[45] be that external or internal. Because concepts cannot present themselves to the mind apart from a linguistic embodiment, because reason cannot arrange the concepts except through imagining their expressions, and because discourse and dialogue are impossible without expressions,[46] it is necessary that the logician be concerned with expressions, and not because expressions in themselves are his primary aim of investigation. If it were possible, we are told, to grasp the concepts free from their expressions, this would be sufficient for the study of logic; and if it were possible for the logician to replace the use of expressions in dialogue by another means, this, too, must be done. But neither of these is possible.[47]

But Ibn Sīnā is convinced that a study of expressions is nothing but a study of the concepts for which the expressions stand.[48] Due to this conviction on his part, it is often difficult to distinguish his use of "expressions" from his use of "concepts." This is made clear, for example, in his discussion of definition, which is a certain form of expression. There he says that a definition includes the essential parts of the concept of the essence; while he should have said that it

---

[43] Conception in the imagination is not abstract, i.e., it is accompanied by matter; while conception in the intellect is abstract, i.e., it is free from matter.
[44] *Naj.*, p. 11.
[45] *Sh. Mad.*, p. 22.
[46] Ibid., p. 23.
[47] Ibid., p. 22.
[48] Ibid., p. 23.

includes parts that signify the essential parts of the concept of the essence.

Ibn Sīnā's procedure, therefore, is to start with a discussion of simple elements, i.e., single expressions, followed by a discussion of valid and invalid forms of the explanatory phrase. The first two methods are devoted exclusively to this. From the Third to the Sixth Method, the way is prepared for a discussion of proof by focusing on propositions, the parts of the proof. The Seventh, Eighth, Ninth and Tenth Methods center on the valid and invalid forms of the proof. Let us, therefore, follow his steps and begin by discussing single expressions.

5. SINGLE EXPRESSIONS

*a. The expression as a sign for the concept*: The expression signifies the concept in one of three ways: (1) by correspondence (*al-muṭābiqa*), as "human being" signifies "rational animal." Here there is total parallelism between the concept signified "rational animal" and the signifying expression "human being." (2) By implication (*at-taḍammun*), as "human being" signifies "animal." Here the concept signified is only a part of the concept for which the signifying expression stands. Or (3) by necessity of following (*al-iltizām*), as "human being" signifies "capacity for laughter," or "capacity for crying." Here the concept signified is not a part of the concept for which the signifying expression stands, but an inseparable external part.

*b. Single and composite expressions*: A single expression is one whose parts cannot have signification as long as they are its parts. We are told that some scholars, whose identity is not revealed, think that a qualification here must be added, namely that the parts of a single expression do not signify anything of the whole of the concept for which the expression stands; but that they may signify something outside this concept. Ibn Sīnā's reply is that this qualification is not needed for completing his notion of a single expression, but perhaps for making it better understood.[49] For he had already stated that inasmuch as the parts of a single expression are parts of such an expression, they do not signify anything. This excludes them from

---

[49] Ibid., pp. 25-26.

being parts of a composite expression, for example – the nature of a composite expression will soon be discussed – or separate expressions.

The qualification that Ibn Sīnā makes is whether or not the part of an expression signifies something depends on the speaker's intention. If the speaker does not intend the part to signify something, then the expression is composite.

The question: "How can the hearer distinguish a single from a composite expression, since the intention of the speaker is not accessible to him?" is not touched upon. But if it were asked of Ibn Sīnā, he may resort to convention, as it is usual for him to do when confronted with similar linguistic problems. In attempting to solve such problems, Ibn Sīnā usually relies on the intention of the speaker and on convention.[50] But since it is the intention of the speaker that is in question here, he is left with convention.

A composite expression, on the other hand, is one whose parts can have signification. Composite expressions are, in turn, divided into two kinds: complete and incomplete. A complete expression is one in which every part has separate signification, as does the verb and the noun. An incomplete expression is one in which there is at least one part which does not have signification, except by means of the rest of the expression. This part is the particle, such as "under" and "not." The noun signifies a concept; and the verb signifies a concept and its temporal determination; and the particle has no separate signification.

Single expressions are not useful for moving from the known to the unknown. Only very few objects can become known in conception through a single expression; and even there the conception of such objects is deficient and bad. The majority of such objects become known through composite expressions.[51] Nor can one move from a single expression to assent, an important tool for getting from the known to the unknown. That is because in order for a single expression to lead to assent, it must be able to cause affirmation and negation; but a single expression cannot do both, otherwise it would be and not be. But this is impossible. Thus affirmation and negation must be caused by something external, yet joined to the single

---

[50] See, for example, the Third Method, note 27.
[51] *Sh. Mad.*, p. 21.

expression. However, when this happens, the expression is no longer single.[52]

c. *Individual and universal expressions*: An individual expression is one which cannot be stated of more than one thing, whether potentially or actually. A universal expression is one which can be so stated, whether potentially, actually or in conception. "This cat" and "John" are examples of individual expressions. "Cat," "spherical figure enclosing the twelve pentagonal sides of a regular dodecahedron" and "sun" are examples of universal expressions – the first actually, the second potentially and the third in conception. Ibn Sīnā expects that one may object saying: what about expressions like: "John" or "Zayd"? Why are they not universal expressions since they apply to many individuals? Here is Ibn Sīnā's response: even though many share in the expression "Zayd," they do so, not in the concept that corresponds to this or that "Zayd," but only in the utterance[53] of this expression.[54]

According to Ibn Sīnā, a logician should be primarily concerned with universal expressions; for one thing there is an infinite number of individual expressions, something which would make their study impossible. And even if their study were possible, it would not help us complete our wisdom,[55] which can be completed only by grasping the essences of things. Ibn Sīnā is convinced that individual expressions do not signify concepts of separate realities. Therefore, a study of them would be superfluous. In the last analysis, only a study of universal expressions will lead to an understanding of the natures of things, which are the ultimate objects of knowledge. Individual expressions, on the other hand, stand for more than the concepts that represent the natures of things, i.e., they also signify the proper accidents of the individual; and thus are apt to confuse the mind as to the realities of things. The expression "Zayd" does not only signify "human being," which is the nature of Zayd, but also a certain height, weight, color, posture, etc.

This is not to say that the logician should not be interested in any type of accident, but only in universal accidents; and in these, only in

---

[52] Ibid.
[53] The word Ibn Sīnā uses here is "*al-masmū'*" (the audible).
[54] *Sh. Mad.*, p. 27.
[55] Ibid., pp. 27-28.

so far as they help us determine the natures of things, as we will soon see. With this in mind, we can now move to an investigation of universal expressions.

*d. Universal expressions (the predicables):* Of universal expression there are three main types: (A) that which is essential, (B) that which is accidental, yet unavoidably attaches to the subject, and (C) that which is accidental, and which is separable from the subject.

(A) The term "essential" is used by Ibn Sīnā to refer to the constituents of the essence; that is, to that which cannot be removed from the essence, without, at the same time, leaving the essence other than what it was. In other words, "essential" refers to that without which the essence cannot be conceived as it is. Examples are "animal" and "rational" for "human being."

It must be mentioned, however, that there are some non-constitutive universals which are also said to be elements without which the essence cannot be conceived. These are the necessary concomitants. Ibn Sīnā is critical of those who are unable to see that there are some elements other than the constituents, without which the essence cannot be conceived.[56] But this must not be taken to mean that the elimination of such necessary concomitants leads to the elimination of the essence: but that their removal indicates that there is no essence to which they attach. If there is no "capacity for laughter" then there is no "human being." The removal of the essence itself is caused by one or more of its internal elements. Thus while necessary concomitants resemble the essentials in that the essence cannot be conceived without them, they differ in that the removal of the former indicates that the essence has been removed but the removal of the latter causes the removal of the essence.

"Essential" is also used to refer to the species as a constituent of the reality of the individual. As "animal" is a constituent of the reality "human being," so also "human being" is a constituent of the reality of "John."

In both of the above senses of "essential" the term is used to refer to a constituent. The difference between the two is that the constituent referred to in the first case is a constituent of a universal reality, while in the second case it is a constituent of an individual.

---

[56] *Ish.*, Part I, p. 164.

Ibn Sīnā emphasizes that "essential" in the sense of "constituent" should not be confused with "essence." The former is an indispensable part of the essence, while the latter is the totality of such parts.

(B) The concomitant accidental is that quality which necessarily attaches to the essence – by virtue of the essence – yet without being a constituent of the essence. It is such qualities that have been said to share with the essentials the fact that they cannot be removed from the conception of the essence. It is perhaps for this reason that these qualities have also been said to be "essential." However, it should be remembered that they are essential accidents, and not purely essential. It must also be noted that Ibn Sīnā reserves the term "essential" in the logic of *al-Ishārāt wat-Tanbīhāt* for the first type of "essential" that has been mentioned, i.e., to that which is a constituent of the essence or reality. Here are two examples of the concomitant accidental: "equality of angles to two right angles" for "triangle" and "capacity for laughter" for "human being."

(C) The separable accidental differs from the essential in that it is not a constituent of the essence; and it differs from the concomitant accidental in that it does not necessarily attach to the essence; and hence it can be eliminated from the conception of the essence.

Now that this has been said, let us now consider which universals belong to which of the above-mentioned three categories. All in all, there are five universals: the genus, the species, the difference, the property and the common accident. Of these, the first three are essential, yet their essentiality is relative. The genus and the difference are essential in relation to the species for they are constituents of it. "Animal" and "rational" which are the genus and the difference for "human being," respectively, are constituents of "human being," and, therefore, are essential with respect to it. The species, on the other hand, is a constitutive element of the concrete individuals subsumed under it, and is, therefore, essential with respect to them. But even though the genus and the difference are essential with respect to the species, they nevertheless play different roles with respect to it: the genus informs us that there is a common nature between the species and all other species that fall under that genus. The difference informs us that there is a distinction between the species and all other species that fall under the same genus. "Animality" presents to us "human being," "horse" and "cat" as sharing in one nature, i.e., "animality." "Rationality," on the other hand, presents to us "human being" as different from any other animal species. It is for this reason that the genus is said to answer the question: "What is it?" for it gives us the general nature of all the species that are subordinate to it. However, according to Ibn Sīnā, it is not inasmuch as the genus is an element of the species that the genus answers this question, but only inasmuch as the species is considered under the aspect of being an instance of the genus.

The difference is said to answer the question, "Which thing is it?" for it distinguishes a species of the same genus.

Now, what of the species? It presents all the individuals that are subordinate to it as having the same kind of nature, even though differing in number. That is why it, too, is said to answer the question, "What is it?" for it presents the individual of a certain species as having the same specific nature as any other individual falling under the same species.

Both property and the common accident are accidental, i.e., they are not constituents of the essence. But, as mentioned, the accidental is of two types: that which is inseparable from the essence and that which is separable. Again, property, which Ibn Sīnā identifies as a universal quality belonging to one universal subject only, divides into that which is inseparable and that which is separable. Ibn Sīnā agrees with Porphyry[57] that the Ancients used the term property in four senses:

(1) That which belongs to a subject, and not to it alone, as "two-footed" belongs to "human being."

(2) That which belongs to all the members of the subject at all times, such as, "capacity for laughter" for "human being."

(3) That which belongs to some members of the subject, such as "peasantry" for "human being."

(4) That which belongs to all the members of the subject, but only for some time, such as, "youth" for "human being."[58]

Ibn Sīnā considers (1) as "unreal property," and (2) to (4) as kinds of "real property." He thus dismisses (1), and discusses only the remaining three kinds, concentrating on (2) which, according to him,

---

[57] Porphyry, *Isagoge*, ed. and trans. Edward W. Warren (Toronto: Pontifical Institute of Mediaeval Studies, 1975), p. 48.

[58] *Sh. Mad.*, pp. 83-84.

is the best kind of real property. Only that property belongs to all the members of the subject, and always is inseparable from the essence and hence cannot be removed from the conception of the essence.

The common accident, which Ibn Sīnā identifies as that quality which belongs to the subject and to others, is also either inseparable or separable. The inseparability of certain common accidents is, however, only in existence. This is exemplified by "black" for "crow." In conception, you can free "crow" from "black": you can imagine him blue or white, without changing his essence. But in actual existence, "crow" can never be other than "black."

A separable accident is something like "two hundred pounds weight" for "this man." This kind of common accident is separable even in existence: "this man" could be "one hundred seventy-five pounds weight" next month.

All of this equips us with knowledge of the simple elements of the explanatory phrase and the parts of the proof. Thus we can now proceed to the explanatory phrase.

## 6. The Explanatory Phrase

Ibn Sīnā discusses two kinds of the explanatory phrase: (1) definition and (2) description.

(1) The definition is a phrase which signifies the essence of a thing. Since the essence has certain constituents, the definition must have parts that indicate these constituents. In other words, the definition signifies the essence through signifying its constituents by implication. Take, for example, the essence of "human being." Its constituents are that which is common to it and to other things under the same genus, i.e., the genus, "animal," and that which is proper to it, i.e., the difference "rational." The definition of "human being" must, therefore, indicate "animal" and "rational." Thus this definition would be "rational animal."

Now what if there were a simple essence, i.e., an essence which cannot be composed of a genus and at least one difference? Such an essence must be, according to Ibn Sīnā, indefinable. For every definable must be in concept a composite of both a genus and at least one difference. It follows that Ibn Sīnā's God, being a simple reality, must be indefinable. The same is true of whatever has no essence. For such an entity, there could only be an expression that indicates the meaning of its name.[59]

If a certain essence has more than one difference, for the definition to signify this essence, it must indicate all its differences. If, on the other hand, it indicates one of them only, then the identifying phrase provides an essential distinction between this essence and others falling under the same genus, or in existence at large; but it could not signify this essence. The example given by Ibn Sīnā is "animal" which has two differences: "sensible" and "moves voluntarily." If you were to say, for example, "animal is a sensible ensouled body" – "ensouled body" being the genus of "animal" – you would have made an essential distinction between "animal" and every other "ensouled body." But you would not have given a definition. Sometimes Ibn Sīnā refers to such an identifying phrase as "definition." It must be remembered, though, that this is not a definition in the real sense.

To recapitulate, the definition is a phrase which determines the essence by means of indicating all the common and proper constituents. Neither more nor less than this can enter the definition. Thus no accident of any sort can be represented in the definition; nor is it appropriate to represent one difference only, when more than one belongs to the essence.

(2) Like the definition, the description is a phrase that signifies the genus by implication, but it differs from the definition in that it has no part that signifies the difference or differences. Instead, it has parts that signify the properties that attach to the essence. The following are examples of description: "Human being is an animal with the capacity to laugh, the capacity to cry, and with broad nails," and "Triangle is a figure with three angles."

What is not clear from Ibn Sīnā is whether all properties must be represented in the description. The examples of description he gives clearly show that the representation of some properties is sufficient. We know, according to Ibn Sīnā, that "human being" has many more properties than those listed in the first example of description, given above. Examples of such properties are "capacity for writing," "walking on two feet" and "peasantry." Two points must here be made. First, all the properties mentioned in the examples of

---

[59] *Sh. Bur.*, p. 281.

description given by Ibn Sīnā are examples of properties that belong to all the members of the species at all times. Second, even though Ibn Sīnā seems willing to call identifying phrases which include only some properties, of the type just mentioned, "descriptions," it would seem reasonable to assume that such phrases are descriptions, yet not in a real sense. A description in a real sense must be one in which all such properties are represented. This would fit in with Ibn Sīnā's view of definition.

In short, a description in the real sense is one in which the genus as well as all properties that belong to the subject at all times are represented.

These are the proper forms of the definition and the description. But, as mentioned, there are improper forms. Seven such forms are enumerated by Ibn Sīnā:

(1) Unfamiliarity of expressions employed in identification. Since the purpose of the identification is to get from the known to the unknown, the identification would defeat its purpose if it were also to begin with what is unknown.

(2) Identifying a thing by means of that which is of an equal epistemic state, i.e., by that which is equally known or equally unknown.

(3) Identifying a thing by what is more unknown than that which is being identified.

(4) Identifying a thing by itself (circular identification).

(5) Identifying a thing by something which cannot be identified except by what is being identified (indirect circular identification.)

(6) Identifying a thing by mentioning what is unnecessary.

(7) Identifying a thing by its correlative. This mistake is due to one's inability to distinguish the following two statements: "When A is known, B is known," and "When A is known, it is known by B." While the former statement is true of correlatives, the latter is not.

7. ON PROPOSITIONS

The discussion concerning propositions divides into four parts: (a) the nature and kinds of propositions, (b) the matters and modes of propositions, (c) contradiction and conversion and (d) propositions involving assent and those resembling them.

*a. The nature and kinds of propositions*: A proposition is a phrase which is either true or false. Of this there are two main types: (A) predicative propositions (Aristotle's categorical propositions) and (B) conditional propositions which in turn divide into (a) connective conditional propositions (the Stoic conditional propositions) and (b) disjunctive conditional propositions (the Stoic disjunctive propositions).

(A) A predicative proposition is a phrase in which an idea is asserted of another – the former idea is called the "predicate" and the latter the "subject." The assertion takes place by means of what is called the "copula." Such a proposition is either affirmative or negative: "A is B," or "A is not B." The latter type of proposition, however, should not be confused with "A is non-B." For here the negative particle is a part of the predicate, and does not negate the copula, as it does in a negative predicative proposition.

A predicative proposition is either definite, indefinite or singular. A definite proposition is either universal or particular. A definite proposition is preceded by a sign (quantity indicator) that indicates whether the judgment applies to all the members of the subject, or only to some. In the first case the judgment is said to be universal, and in the second it is said to be particular. As for the indefinite proposition, there is no sign to indicate whether the judgment in it applies to all the members of the subject, or only to some. And thus the judgment can be taken either universally or particularly. The fact that the subject of the indefinite proposition is universal does not necessitate the universality of the judgment. And finally, a singular proposition is one which, like the indefinite one, is not preceded by any sign; but differs from it in that its subject is an individual.

Thus, we get eight kinds of predicative propositions:

(1) affirmative universal (A proposition),
(2) negative universal (E proposition),
(3) affirmative particular (I proposition),
(4) negative particular (O proposition),
(5) affirmative indefinite,
(6) negative indefinite,
(7) affirmative singular, and
(8) negative singular.

According to Ibn Sīnā, both indefinite and singular propositions must be discarded from science; for the former is confusing, and the latter is not useful.[60] Indefinite propositions are confusing because, as mentioned, it is not clear whether the judgment is universal or particular. And singular propositions are not useful, because, as stated earlier, the ultimate purpose of a human being is to achieve knowledge of the essences. Singular propositions enable us to acquire knowledge only about individuals, which are collections of accidents attached to essences.

(B) A conditional proposition is one whose main parts were originally propositions. But they have lost the quality of being propositions, after having been attached to particles such as "if-then" or "either-or." It is the whole conditional that counts as a proposition. This is a point on which Ibn Sīnā puts a great emphasis.

(a) A conditional proposition whose parts are attached to if-then, is a connective conditional. Here the part of the connective conditional which plays the role of the predicate (the consequent) is not asserted of that which plays the role of the subject (the antecedent). Rather, it is said either to follow necessarily from it, or to attach to it by chance.

(b) A conditional proposition whose constituents are attached to "either-or" is a disjunctive conditional. Again, that which plays the role of the predicate (the consequent) is not asserted of that which plays the role of the subject (the antecedent). Rather, the consequent is said to be in conflict with the antecedent.

Of disjunctive propositions, there are two types: the real disjunctive and the unreal disjunctive.

The real disjunctive is one in which the parts of the proposition are exclusive of each other: they cannot be true, nor can they both be false. As for the unreal disjunctive, it is either one in which the parts can all be true, but they cannot all be false; or they can all be false, but they cannot all be true. It is clear, then, that the definition of a disjunctive proposition given by Ibn Sīnā, namely that it is one whose parts are in conflict, applies to the real disjunctive only.

It is because the whole of the conditional and not its parts constitutes a proposition, that Ibn Sīnā treats conditional propositions in the same manner he treats predicative ones. Thus similar to predicative propositions, conditional propositions can be either affirmative or negative. And also similar to them, they can be either

---

[60] *Tr. Log.*, p. 24.

definite or indefinite. The definite are preceded by a quantity indicator, and the indefinite are not. The following are examples of definite connective conditionals:

"Whenever the sun is out, then it is day" (A proposition).

"It is never the case that if the sun is out, then it is night" (E proposition).

"Sometimes when the sun is out, the sky is cloudy" (I proposition).

"It is not the case that whenever the sun is out, then it is cloudy" (O proposition).

And the following are examples of definite disjunctive conditionals:

"Always this number is even, or it is odd" (A proposition).

"It is never the case that either the sun is out, or it is day" (E proposition).

"Sometimes, Zayd is in the house, or 'Amr is in the house" (I proposition).

"It is not the case that either fever is choleric, or it is inflammatory" (O proposition).

It is true that Ibn Sīnā's predicative propositions are those of Aristotle, and his conditional propositions were already present in Stoic logic; but his equal treatment of the predicative and conditional propositions shows independence from these two schools. His discussion of conditional propositions with respect to quality and quantity is, for example, a mark of originality. In this Nicholas Rescher testifies: "So far as I have been able to determine, Avicenna is the first writer in the history of logic to give an analysis of hypothetical and disjunctive propositions that is fully articulated with respect to quality and to quantity.[61]

*b. The matters and modes of propositions*: Earlier we spoke of the concepts in a phrase as its matter. But "matter" is also used in the sense of the subject-predicate relation. (Remember that since the conditional proposition is treated by Ibn Sīnā in the same manner as a predicative one, whatever is said here of the subject-predicate relation also holds for the antecedent-consequent relation). The predicate attaches to the subject either in a manner which cannot be otherwise

---

[61] Nicolas Rescher, *Studies in the History of Arabic Logic* (Pittsburgh: University of Pittsburgh Press, 1963), p. 83.

(necessity of existence) or in a manner which can be otherwise (possibility) or in a manner which cannot but be otherwise (impossibility: necessity of non-existence) – the first and third are subsumed under the name "necessity."

When this relation is an internal state of the proposition, apart from expression, it is the matter of the proposition. But this state can be made explicit in language, and as such, it is the mode of the proposition. Thus we get three modes: necessity of existence, possibility and impossibility.

While it is impossible, in reality, for the predicate not to have one of these three relations to the subject, in expression, it is possible to affirm or deny the predicate of the subject, without expressing the manner of their relation. That is, you can say "A is B," without attention as to whether or not this can be otherwise. Such a statement is called "absolute" or "non-modal."

Since a discussion of necessity and possibility will prove important for an understanding of demonstration later on, we will give a brief sketch of this discussion.

Necessity is of two main types: (A) eternal or absolute (not conditioned), and (B) conditioned necessity which is, in turn, of several kinds: (a) conditioned by the existence of the essence of the subject; (b) conditioned by the duration of the subject's being qualified by a certain quality; (c) conditioned by the duration of the predicate; (d) conditioned by a determined time; and (e) conditioned by a non-determined time.

(A) and (Ba) are the only kinds of real necessity. The necessity of (b) through (e) is unreal. And propositions that involve this kind of necessity are called "concrete." Concrete propositions together with those involving duration without necessity are called "non-necessary" or "absolute." Remember, though, that "absolute" in this sense is not "absolute" in the sense of "non-modal." Unfortunately, it is often the case that Ibn Sīnā mentions "absolute" without specifying in what sense he is using the term "absolute." This creates additional difficulties and requires careful attention.

As for possibility, it divides into the following kinds:

(A) The negation of impossibility. (This is "possibility" in the common or general sense.)

(B) The negation of impossibility as well as the negation of the necessity of existence. (This is "possibility" in the real or proper sense.) Necessity of existence is subsumed under "possibility" in the first sense, but it is excluded from "possibility" in the second sense. However, unreal necessity is subsumed under the latter kind of possibility.

(C) The negation of any kind of necessity. (This is "possibility" in the most proper sense.)

(D) The negation of future necessity.

*c. Contradiction and conversion*: Two propositions are contradictory if one is true and the other false. A number of conditions must be satisfied in order for contradiction to obtain.

(A) The meaning of the parts of the one proposition must be the same as that of the parts of the other, and both must be under the same states. If, for example, you say "John has seen a red *'ayn*" and "John has not seen a red *'ayn*," and you mean by the first "*'ayn*" "eye," and by the second "*'ayn*" "water fountain," then you would not have made two contradictory statements. Or if you say "John writes" and "John does not write," and you meant by the first "write" "write in potentiality," and by the second "write" "write in actuality," again you would not have made two contradictory statements.

(B) If the propositions are definite, then one of them must be universal and the other particular.

(C) One of the propositions must be affirmative and the other negative.

But these conditions are not sufficient to bring about contradiction between two absolute propositions, whether "absolute" is taken in the general or in the concrete sense. Rather, what is further needed is a specification of time in one of the propositions, such that the time of the truth of one overlaps with the time of the falsity of the other.

Let us first take "absolute" in the general sense, and say "Absolutely, every A is B." The contradictory of this proposition is: "Some A is always not B." For the first proposition does not specify a time of the truth of this proposition. This means that while this proposition may be true now, it may not be true tomorrow. Rather, its contrary: "Absolutely, no C is B" may be true tomorrow. And thus "Absolutely, some C is not B" may be true with "Absolutely, every C is B." Because an absolute proposition taking "absolute" in the general sense, is free from the element of time, its contradictory must be a proposition applicable to all times.

Also, if "absolute" is taken in the concrete sense, an absolute proposition is contradicted by a proposition applicable to all times. While an absolute proposition in the first sense does not specify any time, an absolute proposition in the present sense specifies "some time." If, for example, you say, "Concretely, every C is B," what you are saying is that for some time, every C is B. But again, "For some time, some C is not B" may be true with this proposition. The contradictory of "Concretely (for some time), every C is B" must, therefore, be "Some C is always B or it is always not B." This is the same as saying "Not concretely, some C is B."

Similarly, the contradictory of any other affirmative modal proposition is one in which the mode is negated, and not one in which the proposition itself is negated. The contradictory of "Necessarily every C is B" is "Not necessarily, every C is B." And the contradictory of "Necessarily, no C is B" is "Not necessarily, no C is B."

Conversion is making the subject a predicate and the predicate a subject, with the retention of the quality and the truth or falsity of the proposition. Again, Ibn Sīnā discusses the conversion of non-modal and modal propositions.

In specific absoluteness, a universal negative proposition converts to itself. However, this is so only under the following condition: when the absolute proposition is of the type which involves necessity of the subject's being qualified by the quality accompanying it.[62] For it is only here that if, for example, "No movable changes as long as it moves" then "Nothing of that which changes moves as long as it moves." But in a proposition whose absoluteness is general, while "No A is B" may be true, "No B is A" may be false. That is because the predicate may be more general than the subject.

An absolute universal affirmative proposition, taking "absolute" in the concrete sense, converts to a particular affirmative. An absolute particular affirmative converts to itself. And a necessary particular negative does not convert.

A necessary universal negative converts to itself. A necessary universal affirmative converts to a particular affirmative. A necessary particular affirmative converts to itself. And a necessary particular negative does not convert.

---

[62] *Naj.*, p. 28.

Finally, a possible universal negative does not convert. A possible universal affirmative converts to a particular affirmative. A possible particular affirmative converts to itself. And a possible particular negative does not convert.

*d. Propositions involving assent and those resembling them*: In *an-Majāt*, nine types of propositions involving assent are listed:[63]

(1) Sensible propositions: these are propositions whose assent is derived from external senses only.

(2) Experiential propositions: these are propositions which are the result of the retention of repeated sense experience, whether this experience is of the external or the internal sense – propositions of these two types of experience will be classified in *al-Ishārāt wat-Tanbīhāt* under "observational propositions."

(3) Propositions based on unanimous traditions: these are propositions in which assent is derived from multiple testimonies.

(4) Received propositions: these are propositions whose assent is derived from scholars or respected religious leaders.

(5) Estimative propositions: these are propositions in which assent is derived from the estimative power. They are false if their subject is non-sensible; and true if their subject is sensible.

(6) Widespread propositions: these are propositions whose assent is derived from their being widely-known. They are either primary propositions – these are true; or propositions based on notoriety – these may be true or false.

(7) Presumed propositions: these are propositions whose assent is derived from a strong inclination of the soul with a conviction of the mind that the opposite is possible.

(8) Imagined propositions: these propositions produce a strong effect on the soul, because of their resemblance to primary or widely-known propositions. Imagined propositions do not involve assent in a primary sense, but only secondarily, inasmuch as they resemble those that involve assent. That is why, in some places, they are classified as propositions that do not involve assent,[64] and in other places, such as in *an-Najāt*, they are classified under propositions that involve assent. It must be remembered, though, that they are said not to involve

---

[63] Ibid., pp. 60-66.
[64] *Sh. Bur.*, p. 63.

assent in a primary manner, and to involve assent in a secondary manner.

(9) Primary propositions: these propositions derive their assent from the essence of a clear intellect, so that, whenever their terms are grasped by the intellect, a judgment is made.

All of these are given as propositions involving assent without mediation.[65] That is, one can accept these propositions without having to go back to other propositions.

In *al-Ishārāt wat-Tanbīhāt*, this list of propositions is given with some variation. Here are the kinds listed:

(1) Primary propositions.

(2) Observational propositions: these differ from the sensible propositions listed in *an-Najāt*, in that they do not only include propositions derived from external senses – as do the sensible propositions, but also propositions derived from the internal senses – the latter being propositions concerning our knowledge of ourselves, our acts, fears, etc.

(3) Experiential propositions.

(4) Intuited propositions: notice that these propositions are not listed in *an-Najāt*. It is not clear from *al-Ishārāt wat-Tanbīhāt* what intuited propositions are. All that we are told is that they are "propositions in which the principle of the judgment is a very strong intuition of the soul, with which doubt is removed and to which the mind submits." [66] But what is an intuition? The answer is found in *al-Burhān*: "It is such that if the object sought is presented to the mind, the middle term is also presented without search." [67]

(5) Propositions based on unanimous traditions.

(6) Propositions containing syllogisms: these are missing from the list in *an-Najāt*. They are described in *al-Ishārāt wat-Tanbīhāt* as "propositions in which assent is made only due to an intermediary. That intermediary is not among what escapes the mind – thus requiring the mind to seek it. Rather, whenever the two extreme terms of the problem are present to the mind, the intermediary is also

---

[65] *Naj.*, p. 60.
[66] *Ish.*, Part I, p. 348.
[67] *Sh. Bur.*, pp. 59, 259.

present to it."[68] But the question remains as to how these propositions differ from intuitive propositions.

All the above mentioned propositions are those that must be accepted.

(7) Widely-known propositions.

(8) Estimative propositions.

The above eight kinds of propositions are subsumed under "beliefs."

(9) Propositions based on outside sources: these include received and determined propositions – the latter being either propositions based on the admission of the interlocutor or propositions employed in the premises of the sciences.

The above nine kinds of propositions are called "admitted propositions."

(10) Presumed propositions.

(11) Ambiguous propositions.

(12) Imagined propositions.

It is clear from this that not all propositions involving assent are true propositions, but are propositions which are thought to be true. An arguer can employ any of these propositions in the premises of an argument. However, it is only those propositions involving assent corresponding to the truth, i.e., the certain propositions, that can lead to demonstration, the most assured form of science.

In *an-Najāt* the following propositions are said to be non-certain: widespread propositions, received propositions and presumed propositions. Imagined propositions are not classified under those that are certain or those that are non-certain. The remaining kinds of propositions are classified under those that are certain.[69]

In the *Treatise on Logic* first principle propositions (primary propositions), perceptual propositions (sensible propositions), experimental propositions (experiential propositions) and testimonial ones (propositions based on unanimous traditions) are said to be employed in the premises of the syllogism, a kind of discourse which is said there to give certainty and truth. But it should have been said instead that they are employed in the demonstrative syllogism for it is only

---

[68] *Ish.*, Part I, p. 350.
[69] *Naj.*, p. 66.

this kind of syllogism which is held by Ibn Sīnā to give certainty. Propositions based on authority (received propositions) and propositions based on custom (widely-known propositions) are employed in dialectic, a kind of discourse which, though it does not give certainty, has, nevertheless, the following advantages:

> (1) One can defeat, in argument, those people who pretend to have knowledge, but who are really ignorant to the premises of their argument. (2) One can demonstrate truth to those who do not understand syllogistic reasoning. (3) It is often the case that students of the minor sciences, like medicine, geometry, and natural science, take on faith the principles of their science. The teacher of the metaphysics, the science of sciences, can show these students, by means of dialectic, how the premises of their sciences are derived from metaphysics. (4) One can show what things taken to be true, are false, and what things taken to be false, are true. In so doing, one can alert the student to errors and deficiencies in argument.[70]

Dubious propositions (in *al-Ishārāt wat-Tanbīhāt*, these propositions are said to be those that are ambiguous) and those raised by the imagination (estimative propositions) are employed in sophistical discourse, a kind of discourse which gives no knowledge. Propositions known by authority, those which appear to be known by custom and those raised by our fears and suspicions (it is not clear what the last two kinds of propositions are; it is our guess that "propositions that appear to be known by custom" are "presumed propositions" – our conjecture is based on the fact that in *al-Ishārāt wat-Tanbīhāt*, rhetorical syllogisms are said to employ received propositions and presumed ones) are employed in rhetoric, a kind of discourse used by theologians and politicians. And propositions raised by emotions (imagined propositions) are employed in poetical discourse.[71]

We thought it fit to outline here Ibn Sīnā's discussion of propositions involving assent and those not involving assent as given in *al-Burhān*.[72] This outline will give the reader a different perspective

---

[70] *Tr. Log.*, p. 42.
[71] Ibid.
[72] *Sh. Bur.*, pp. 63-67.

of these propositions. This will be helpful in understanding the Sixth Method and in the study of the syllogism, since in *al-Burhān* the classification of these propositions is made with their being principles of syllogism in mind.

The principles of syllogisms are either:

I. Propositions not involving assent: these are the imagined propositions. The effect they leave on the soul plays the role of that by means of which assent occurs. Such propositions do not have a primary use in syllogisms. They are the principles of poetical syllogisms.

II. Propositions involving assent are either:
  1. Propositions whose assent is necessary; these are either:
    (1) Propositions whose necessity of assent is external; these are:
      (A) sensible propositions;
      (B) experimental propositions; or
      (C) propositions based on unanimous traditions.
    (2) Propositions whose necessity of assent is internal. Internal necessity is either:
      (A) From the intellect; these are either:
        (a) from the intellect by itself; these are the primary propositions which must be accepted.
        (b) from the intellect aided by something else; these are either:

($b^1$) Propositions in which what aids the intellect is something not instinctive to the mind. Assent here is acquired; and thus it is subsequent to the principles. No further mention of this kind is given here, since the present discussion is concerned with principles of syllogisms.

($b^2$) Propositions in which what aids the intellect is something instinctive to the intellect, i.e., whose middle term is present to the natural mind. No further inquiry to acquire it is needed; this kind is called "a premise with a natural syllogism" (*muqaddama fī ṭriyyat al-qiyās*) – in the sense that the middle term of its syllogism is simultaneous with it.

      (B) External to the intellect: propositions whose necessity of assent is external to the intellect are judgments of the estimative power. These are judgments whose necessity is estimative, if they are about matters concerning which the intellect does not have a primary judgment. Such matters are non-sensible. Thus the estimative power obliges the soul to give necessary judgments by considering such matters as if they were sensible. Such necessity is unreal in contrast to that of the intellect. Propositions whose assent is necessary, and which are employed in demonstration, are only those whose necessity of assent is real.

    2. Propositions whose assent is admitted, without their opposite being present in the soul; these are either:

       (1) Propositions whose admission is valid; these are:

          (A) Propositions in which the admission is common; these are:

             (a) Propositions whose admission is based on the opinion of all people. These are accepted widely-known propositions. If they are true, their truth is not made evident by the natural mind. Among these widely-known propositions, there are those that can be true; but in order for them to become certain, they require proof. Among the widely-known propositions, it is also possible to find false propositions. The present kind of propositions, i.e., (a), is the unrestricted kind of widely-known propositions.

             (b) Propositions whose admission is based on the opinion of a group of people are exemplified in propositions whose admission is based on the opinion of religious leaders, or the opinion of the masters of a skill. This kind of propositions is called "restricted widely-known propositions." Of (b), there are also those that are exemplified in propositions whose admission is based on the opinion of one or two individuals, or any limited number of individuals in whom one has confidence. These are called "received propositions."

          (B) Propositions in which the admission is that of one individual. These are useful in syllogisms addressed to that particular individual. Neither the speaker nor the syllogism benefits from them.

       (2) Propositions whose admission is erroneous. These are such that what is admitted in them is admitted to be something else, due to the fact that it resembles something else and shares with it an expression or a meaning. These are the ambiguous propositions.

    3. Presumed propositions are based on opinion, and not certainty. The source of the presumption is either:

       (1) Resemblance to widely-known propositions. Because of this, such presumptive propositions are at first widely-known. But further consideration reveals that they are not widely-known.

(2) The source of the presumption is confidence – but it is not clear, confidence in whom. Presumptive propositions are useful in syllogisms inasmuch as they are accompanied by a belief, and not inasmuch as their opposite is present in the mind.

All the above principles of syllogisms are given by the syllogizer. There are also those that are given by the teacher. These are such that the student is asked to admit something on which evidence for something else is established. Thus the student posits them. These are called "posited principles" and "postulates."

## 8. THE PROOF

Analogy, induction and syllogism are the three types of proof listed by Ibn Sīnā.

(1) Analogy is a judgment about a particular thing, based on the similarity between that particular thing and another. Here is an example:

> The world is originated, because it is a composite body resembling a building.
> A building is originated.
> Therefore, the world is originated.[73]

Four elements are involved in analogy:

(1) the fundamental: that which is said to be resembled, such as "building," in the above-mentioned example;

(2) the branch: that which is said to resemble, such as "world" in our example;

(3) the common idea or cause: that which is shared by the fundamental and the branch, such as "composite body" in the present example; and

(4) the judgment about the branch, such as "originated" in the same example.

Analogy is the weakest form of proof, because it is a judgment about a particular thing; and we know that such judgments do not count as scientific in Ibn Sīnā's view. Further, analogy can never give

---

[73] *Naj.*, p. 58.

us certitude. For two particular things that are similar in a certain respect may be different in other respects.[74] It is for these two reasons that Ibn Sīnā dismisses analogy in the sciences.

(2) Induction is a judgment about a universal, derived from judgments about particular cases of that subject. Induction is a more reliable form of proof than analogy, because the subject of the former is a universal while the subject of the latter is an individual. Still induction is not classified in our text as a correct science. It should be remembered, though, that there are two kinds of induction: complete induction and incomplete induction – the latter being the more common[75] and the better known.[76] In complete induction, the judgment applies to every member of the class.[77] The conclusion of this kind of induction is certain.[78] That is why this kind of induction is said to be demonstrative.[79] In incomplete induction, the judgment applies only to the majority of the members of the class.[80] Here the conclusion is probable.[81] It is incomplete induction that Ibn Sīnā has in mind when he says that induction is not a correct science. This is the only kind mentioned in *al-Ishārāt wat-Tanbīhāt*.

(3) Like Aristotle, Ibn Sīnā considers the syllogism as the most reliable form of proof.[82] And like him, he defines the syllogism as a discourse, consisting of propositions which when laid down necessarily lead to another proposition.

Syllogisms are of two main kinds: (A) conjunctive syllogisms and (B) repetitive syllogisms.

(A) A conjunctive syllogism is defined by Ibn Sīnā as one in which neither the conclusion nor its contradictory is actually stated in the premises. As we will soon see, this main feature clearly distinguishes the conjunctive syllogism from the repetitive syllogism. It is because

---

[74] *Tr. Log.*, p. 38.
[75] Ibid.
[76] *Naj.*, p. 58.
[77] Ibid.
[78] *Sh. Bur.*, p. 79; *Tr. Log.*, p. 38.
[79] *Sh. Bur.*, p. 55.
[80] *Naj.*, p. 58.
[81] *Tr. Log.*, p. 38.
[82] Ibid., p. 29.

the premises of this kind of syllogism are conjoined by the particle "and" that it has come to be called "conjunctive."

There are three kinds of conjunctive syllogisms:

(a) that which consists of predicative propositions;
(b) that which consists of conditional propositions, which can be either:
  ($b^1$) that which consists of connective conditionals; or
  ($b^2$) that which consists of disjunctive conditionals; or
  ($b^3$) that which is a mixture of connective and disjunctive conditionals; and
(c) that which is a mixture of predicative and conditional propositions.

(a) It has been said that a syllogism is one in which the conjunction of the premises necessarily leads to a conclusion. In order to point out the clarity of the evidence for this necessity of following of the conclusion, and the conditions for this necessity, four types of predicative syllogisms are distinguished:

(1) one in which the middle term is a predicate of both the minor premise and a subject of the major;

(2) one in which the middle term is a predicate of both the minor and the major premises;

(3) one in which the middle term is a subject of both the minor and major premises; and

(4) one in which the middle term is a subject of the minor premise and a predicate of the major.

These are known, respectively, as first, second, third and fourth figures – a figure being a syllogism whose form of the conjecture of premises is based on the manner of placing the middle term in relation to the other two terms.

The necessity with which the conclusion of the first figure follows from the conjunction of the premises is evident. That is why this figure is said to be perfect. The second and third figures (classified in the text as the third and fourth figures) are not as good as the first; for in them, this necessity of following is not immediately evident. However, they are accepted because they can be made to achieve the degree of evidence exhibited by the first figure, by reducing them to the first figure. This can be done by converting one of their premises.

The case of the fourth figure is harder. It takes the conversion of both premises to achieve this degree of evidence and perfection. It is for this reason that Ibn Sīnā, while admitting the fourth figure, puts it aside as not worthy of treatment.

In *al-Ishārāt wat-Tanbīhāt*, only one condition is said to apply to the three figures: that the two premises cannot both be particular.

(b) Figures, similar to those formed in predicative conjunctive syllogisms, are also formed in conditional conjunctive syllogisms. Ibn Sīnā mentions only the first three figures of conditional conjunctive syllogisms, the only worthwhile figures according to him. The rules governing these figures are said to be the same as those governing predicative conjunctive syllogisms.

In *al-Ishārāt wat-Tanbīhāt*, there is hardly any discussion of conditional conjunctive syllogisms. And no examples are given of such syllogisms. The reason seems to be that first Ibn Sīnā feels that he had already exhausted the subject in *al-Qiyās* and in *an-Najāt*; and second, *al-Ishārāt wat-Tanbīhāt* is more of a summary of his views. That is why it should include his main important ideas. This is an indication that even though he admits that conditional syllogisms can be conjunctive, and criticizes those who are not willing to make this admission,[83] he, nevertheless, does not consider them as important as predicative conjunctive syllogisms, which in *al-Ishārāt wat-Tanbīhāt* he treats at length.

(c) Of syllogisms that are formed of predicative and conditional propositions, *al-Ishārāt wat-Tanbīhāt* offers only some examples, and no discussion.

(B) A repetitive syllogism is one in whose premises either the conclusion or its contradictory is mentioned. A repetitive syllogism can be either

(1) a syllogism in whose premises a connective conditional is mentioned, or

(2) a syllogism in whose premises a disjunctive conditional is mentioned.

Of (1) there are only two valid forms, as exemplified in the following two statements "If A, then B; A; therefore, B," and "If A, then B; not B; therefore, not A."

---

[83] *Ish.*, Part I, p. 375.

In (2) the disjunctive mentioned is either (A) a real disjunctive, or (B) an unreal disjunctive.

In (A) there are two valid forms: one in which whatever part of the disjunctive is repeated, the conclusion is the contradictory of the part of the disjunctive which is not repeated; or one in which whatever part of the disjunctive is denied, the conclusion is the affirmation of the other part. An example of the former is "Either A or B; A; therefore, not B." And an example of the latter is: "Either A or B; not A; therefore B."

And finally, (B) could be either (a) one in which the disjunctive does not permit exclusion of all the parts, or (b) one in which the disjunctive does not permit union of all the parts. The valid form of (a) is a syllogism in which the denial of the repetition of any part of the disjunctive yields the affirmation of the other part as a conclusion: "Either A or B; not B; therefore, A." And the valid form of (b) is a syllogism in which the repetition of any part of the disjunctive yields the contradictory of the other part as a conclusion: "Either A or B; A; therefore, not B." Or "Either A or B; B; therefore, not A."

9. ON DEMONSTRATION

In ancient and medieval times, demonstration was considered a very important, if not the most important, branch of logic. Ibn Sīnā devotes to its discussion a whole part of the logic of *ash-Shifā'*, and takes it up in all of his other logical writings, with the exception of *Manṭiq al-Mashriqiyyīn*. In *al-Ishārāt wat-Tanbīhāt*, the discussion of demonstration is particularly sketchy and difficult to follow. That is why we had to rely heavily on his other logical works, especially *al-Burhān*, in order to understand this discussion.

The following are the main points discussed: a. the nature of demonstration and b. the things on which demonstration is based.

*a. The nature of demonstration*: If the syllogism is the most reliable form of proof, demonstration is the most certain kind of syllogism.[84] A demonstration is a syllogism whose premises must be accepted, i.e., are certain. That is why the conclusion, too, is certain. But it is not because the conclusion is certain that demonstration is called certain; but because the premises are such:

---

[84] *Tr. Log.*, p. 29.

It does not seem to be the case that what is intended by "certain" is that the conclusion of the demonstration is certain. For if its conclusion is certain, this does not mean that it itself is certain .... I am most inclined to believe that what is intended by this is a syllogism composed of certain premises .... For if certainty were of the premises, the demonstration itself would also be certain.[85]

Two points must here be made. First, certainty is of two kinds: that which is always and that which is for some time.[86] Second, "certain" and "necessary" are used by Ibn Sīnā interchangeably. For according to him, what is certain is necessary, and vice versa. Therefore, the premises of the demonstration must be necessary. But then what do we make of Ibn Sīnā's claim that a demonstration can have either necessary premises (from which a necessary conclusion is drawn), possible premises (from which a possible conclusion is drawn) or a mixture of possible and necessary premises (from which a non-necessary conclusion is drawn)?[87]

In order to respond to this difficulty, we must first remember that "certain" or "necessary" are used in the above-mentioned two senses. In addition to this, we must also point out that Ibn Sīnā distinguishes three kinds of possible propositions: (1) that which is possible in the majority of cases, (2) that which is possible in equal cases, and (3) that which is possible in a minority of cases. The first is inclined toward existence, the second is not inclined either toward existence or toward non-existence, and the third is inclined toward non-existence. These possible propositions can be considered from two perspectives: from the perspective of existence and from the perspective of possibility.

Considered from the perspective of existence, only the first kind of possible propositions is certain. However, it must be remembered that "certainty" here is for some time, and is hence, different from that involved in the purely necessary propositions in which certainty is always. Propositions whose possibility is of the second kind are not certain, in any sense, when considered from the perspective of existence. The same is true of propositions whose possibility is of the

---

[85] *Sh. Bur.*, pp. 78-79.
[86] Ibid., p. 78.
[87] *Ish.*, Part I, pp. 450-451 and pp. 466-467.

third kind. Rather, propositions whose possibility is of the third kind are certain when considered from the perspective of non-existence.

If, on the other hand, these possible propositions are considered from the perspective of possibility, all of them would be certain or necessary. For they can never be other than possible. In other words, they are necessarily possible.[88] Therefore, when in *al-Ishārāt wat-Tanbīhāt*, Ibn Sīnā is critical of those who hold that only necessary propositions and those that are possible in the majority of cases are employed in the premises of the demonstration,[89] he is thinking of the other kinds of possible propositions looked at from the perspective of possibility. For even possible propositions whose possibility is in equal cases or that in the minority of cases can be so employed under the aspect of possibility; since, as mentioned, they too are certain under this aspect.

Of demonstration, there are two kinds: (1) causal demonstration and (2) factual demonstration.

(1) A causal demonstration is one in which the cause of the judgment, in reality or existence, as well as in the mind, is given.

(2) A factual demonstration is, on the other hand, one in which only the cause of the judgment in the mind is given.

*b. The things on which demonstration is based*: These are: (A) the principles of demonstration, (B) the subject of demonstration, and (C) the questions in demonstration.

(A) The principles of demonstration are the premises and definitions of which demonstration is composed.

The premises are either (1) propositions that must be accepted – these are employed by the syllogizer; (2) propositions admitted by virtue of confidence in the teacher – these are called posited principles; or (3) propositions admitted with doubt in the student's mind – these are called "postulates." (2) and (3) are employed by the teacher.

As for the definition, it has already been defined as a phrase signifying the essence. However, this is not the kind of definition employed as a principle in demonstration. In *al-Burhān*, four kinds of definitions are listed: (1) the definition that gives the meaning of the

---

[88] *Sh. Bur.*, pp. 248-249.
[89] *Ish.*, Part I, p. 469.

name – this kind of definition does not signify the existence of a thing or the cause of the existence of that thing, and for this reason it is called metaphorical or unreal definition; (2) the definition that signifies the essence[90] – this is a complete or real definition; (3) the definition that gives the cause of the existence of the defined – this is employed as the middle term in a demonstration and since it indicates the cause only, it is called incomplete; and (4) the definition that is an effect of the definition which is a middle term in the demonstration – this fourth kind is a conclusion in a demonstration, but because it indicates the effect only, it is also referred to as incomplete. However, both kinds of incomplete definitions, i.e., (3) and (4), are considered real – the reason being that each of them indicates some aspect of the existence of a thing. (3) is the only kind of definition employed as a principle in a demonstration.[91]

(B) The subject of demonstration is something whose essential accidents are investigated in the science, as one investigates the oneness of God in the divine science.

(C) Regarding the questions in demonstration, there are four principle questions: "Is the thing?" "What is the thing?" "Which is the thing?" and "Why is the thing?" [92] The first of these questions seeks an assent about a thing; the second seeks a conception of a thing; the third seeks a distinction of it; and the fourth seeks the cause of the assent.[93]

The question "Is the thing?" is either simple or compound.[94] In its simple form, this question seeks the non-restricted existence of a thing, as in the statements: "Does God exist (*mawjūd*)?" and "Does

---

[90] In this context, Ibn Sīnā uses "existence" (*wujūd*) and "essence" (*thāt*) interchangeably. Thus the present kind of definition which signifies the essence is described in other places as one which signifies the existence of a thing. However, it is clear that what is intended is the nature or quiddity which is the essence, and not the existence. In fact, the existence of a thing is not indicated at all in this kind of definition. For existence is extrinsic to the essence, and only the essence is indicated. The procedure we have followed is this: when we are either quoting, or giving a close paraphrasing of a passage from Ibn Sīnā, we use the term which he uses, be that "existence" or "essence." However, when we are freely interpreting or commenting on a point, the term we have used is "essence" or "nature."

[91] *Sh. Bur.*, pp. 288-290.
[92] Compare this with Aristotle: *Anal. Post.*, II, 1, 22-35.
[93] *Naj.*, pp. 67-68.
[94] *Sh. Bur.*, p. 68.

the void exist (*mawjūd*)?" For this reason, this form of the question is also called "the non-restricted form of 'Is the thing?'" In its compound form, on the other hand, this question seeks the state or states of a thing as in the statements "Is (*mawjūd*) human being an animal?" or "Is (*mawjūd*) God a creator of the earth?" Because this kind of question seeks an aspect of the thing, it is called "the restricted form of 'Is the thing?'" Notice that "exist" in the simple form of this question, and "is" in the compound form are translations of the same Arabic word "*mawjūd*." That is why it was difficult to render these two forms of the question in English under one name, as they are in Arabic. It must be remembered, though, that when "*mawjūd*" is used in the simple form of this question, it is a predicate, and when it is used in the compound form, it is a copula.

The question "What is the thing?" seeks either the comprehension of the name of a thing, or its essence. An example of the former is "What is the void?" By this is intended "What is meant by the name 'void'?" This question is prior to every other question. For unless you know the meaning of the name employed, it would not make sense for you to ask further questions. An example of the latter is: "What is human being?" By this is intended "What is the essence or nature of 'human being'?" This kind of question is preceded by the simple form of "Is the thing?" [95] For unless you know that a thing exists, it would not make sense to ask about its nature.

The question "Which thing is it?" seeks to distinguish a thing from another, by inquiring about its essential attributes or properties. This question enters in potentiality in the simple form of "Is the thing?"

And finally, the question "Why is the thing?" is divided into two kinds: that which seeks the cause of the assent only, and that which seeks the cause of the existence of a thing.[96]

So far, only valid syllogisms have been discussed. But error may occur in a syllogism, thus rendering it invalid or fallacious. There is no need to discuss such syllogisms here, since Ibn Sīnā's discussion of them in the Tenth Method is sufficiently clear.

What must be mentioned, though, is that this part on logic ends with an address to the reader, which may be summarized as follows. If after paying attention to all that has been said here you make an

---

[95] *Sh. Bur.*, p. 69; *Naj.*, pp. 67-68.
[96] *Naj.*, p. 68.

effort to repeat it, review it and make use of it, yet you still make an error, then you are not fit to pursue wisdom. For whatever one is fit for, one can do with ease.

### III. A WORD ABOUT THE TRANSLATION

In this translation, an attempt has been made to strike some middle ground between a literal rendering, which does not always make sense in English, and a lucid rendering, which does not always capture the meaning intended. The best translation is that which is faithful to the original text and which is at the same time readable. But of course this is not always possible. It is hoped that where the translation has failed in this respect, the introduction and notes will succeed in dispelling the resulting difficulties.

In translating this work, appropriate division into paragraphs, and punctuation (including quotations and parentheses) were added. Brackets mark expressions added to the text. The marginal numbering indicates the page numbers of Dunyā's edition. The reader may notice that often these numbers are not consecutive. The reason is that some pages of this edition do not have any text, but only aṭ-Ṭūsī's *Commentary*. The transition from page to page is indicated by a slash (/). Where a reading different from that of Dunyā is given, this has been indicated in a note, preceded by the word "text." And where the Arabic is cited in a note, without being preceded by the word "text," it is cited not because a different reading is given, but to show the reader what Arabic expression is used. We have found this to be a better procedure than putting the Arabic expressions in parentheses in the text. The latter method, which has often been used by scholars, tends to interrupt the reading and thus could make such a difficult text even more difficult. Finally, Arabic expressions are transliterated in the text, only when the discussion centers around their use in the Arabic language.

# Ibn Sīnā

# Remarks and Admonitions

# Part One: Logic

113 In the name of God, the compassionate, the merciful! In Him we seek help.

114 Praise to God for His good assistance! I appeal to Him for guidance on His way, for inspiration to determine the truth / and for the blessing of His servants whom He has chosen to carry out His message, especially Muḥammad and his family.

For you, who are anxious to determine the truth, I have prepared in these *Remarks and Admonitions* principles and generalities of wisdom. If you are directed by intelligence, it would be easy for you to subdivide them and work out the specific details. /

115 We will start with the science of logic, and from that, move to the science of nature, and then to the prior science.

# The First Method

### Concerning the Purpose of Logic

Logic is intended to give the human being a canonical tool[1] which, if attended to, preserves him from error in his thought. /
I mean by "thought" here that which a human being has, at the point of resolving,[2] to move from things present in his mind — conceptions[3] or assents[4] / (whether scientific, based on opinion, or postulated and already admitted) — / to things not present in it. /
This movement inevitably has order and form in the elements dealt with. Such order and form may occur in a valid or an invalid manner. / Often the invalid manner resembles the valid one, or gives the impression that it resembles it. /
Thus logic is a science by means of which one learns the kinds of movements from elements realized in the human mind to those

---

[1] Logic is a tool for determining the exactness of the sciences by means of alerting one to the principles one needs for acquiring the unknown from the known (*Man.*, p. 5). And it is canonical in the sense that its principles are universal standards against which the conformity of the sciences to them is measured. That is why it is said that logic is a scale (*Qas. Muz.* in *Man.*, p. 3) in the sense that it weighs the conformity of scientific thought to its own principles and thus determines whether this thought is exact or erroneous. In *Naj.*, the relation of logic to thought is said to be analogous to that of grammar to language, and that of the study of meter to poetry (*Naj.*, p. 5). That is, as grammar and meter are two bodies of rules for the determination of the accurateness of the use of language and the creation of poetry, respectively, so also is logic a body of rules for the determination of the accurateness of scientific thought.

[2] *Mā yakūn 'ind ijma' al-insān.*

[3] *Mutaṣawwara.* An object is conceived if it is present in the mind without a judgment.

[4] *Muṣaddaq bihā.* The difference between the object of *taṣawwur* and that of *taṣdīq* is that the former is in the mind free from any judgment while the latter is always accompanied by a judgment. For a discussion of *taṣawwur* and *taṣdīq*, see Harry A. Wolfson, "The Terms of *Taṣawwur* and *Taṣdīq* in Arabic Philosophy and Their Greek, Latin, and Hebrew Equivalents" in *The Moslem World*, 33 (1943), 114-128.

## THE FIRST METHOD

128 whose realization is sought, / the states of these elements, the number of types of order and form in the movements of the mind which occur in a valid manner and the types which are invalid.

129 *Chapter One. Remark: [Concerning the knowledge of the composite as requiring knowledge of single elements]*

Every inquiry that has as its object the order of things so as to move from them to other things or, indeed, that has as its object any composition, requires one to know the single elements[5] of which the

130 order and the composition consist, / although not in every respect but [only] in that respect by virtue of which the order and the composition consist of them validly.

That is why the logician needs to pay attention to certain states of single concepts, and then move from them to pay attention to the states of composition.

131 *Chapter Two: Remark: [Concerning the logician's need for taking into consideration universal language]*

Because there is a certain relation between the expression and the concept, and [because] some states of expressions often affect some states of concepts, the logician must also pay attention to the non-restricted aspect of the expression – insofar as that [aspect] is not restricted to the language of one group of people rather than that of

132 another, / except rarely.

---

[5] *Al-mufradāt.* Even though "*al-mufradāt*" are simple elements in relation to the whole of the phrase of which they are parts, we have preferred to translate this term as "single elements" rather than "simple elements," as some have done (see, for example, Goichon, *Dir. Rem.*, p. 80). Ibn Sīnā obviously knew the word "simple," and if he wished to use it here, he would have done so as he does in other places. Second, there is no need to speak of single expressions as "simple" except if they are truly so; and not all single expressions are such, for some single expressions such as "Abd al-Lāh" are not simple by themselves, as are expressions like "God"; or if they are discussed in relation to the whole of the phrase.

Examples of single elements are: "horse," "neighing," and "animal." But if you were to say, "A horse is a neighing animal," or just "a neighing animal," you would be uttering a composite expression. Since a composite expression is made up of single ones, an understanding of it requires first an understanding of the single expressions. For if you do not understand, for example, what "neighing" and "animal" are, you could not understand what "a neighing animal" is.

## Chapter Three: Remark: [Concerning conception and assent]

133

The unknown corresponds to the known. Thus just as a thing may be known as a pure concept,[6] such as our knowledge of the meaning of the word "triangle," or it may be known as a concept accompanied by assent, such as our knowledge that the angles of every triangle are equal to two right angles,[7] so also a thing may be unknown by way of conception, so that its meaning is not conceived until one learns such [other] concepts, as "the binomial," "the disconnected" and others. /
134 Or it may be unknown as an assent until one learns [another assent], such as that the square on the diagonal is equal to the squares of the
135 sides of the right angle which it subtends.[8] / Thus our path of inquiry
136 concerning the sciences and related studies / either is directed toward a concept sought for realization or is directed toward an assent sought for realization.

It is customary to call the thing by means of which the sought concept is attained "an explanatory phrase,"[9] which includes definition, description, and what resembles them;[10] and to call the thing by means of which the sought assent is attained "proof," which
137 includes syllogism, / induction, and their like.[11]

---

[6] That is, as free from judgment.

[7] Aristotle too had spoken of these two types of knowledge: "The pre-existent knowledge required is of two kinds. In some cases admission of the fact must be assumed, in other comprehension of the meaning of the term used, and sometimes both assumptions are essential. Thus, we assume that every predicate can be either truly affirmed or truly denied of any subject, and that 'triangle' means so and so; as regards 'unit' we have to make the double assumption of the meaning of the word and the existence of the thing" (*Anal. Post.*, I, 1, 71a, 11-15).

[8] *Qawī alā*.

[9] *Qawlan shāriḥan*. By "*qawl*" is meant "any composite expression" (*Naj.*, p. 12). But since a composite expression is any non-single one, be that a phrase – whether complete or incomplete (a discussion of complete and incomplete phrases will follow in Chapter 7 of the present method) – a syllogism, etc., "*qawl*" has, therefore, been translated variably as "phrase," "statement," "discourse," etc., depending on the context.

[10] Such as example (see *Sh. Mad.*, p. 48).

[11] I.e., analogy. It must be mentioned that "and their like" is missing from the present edition. But it is found in Forget's edition (Leyden, 1892, p. 4). Since analogy is one of the types of proof (see *Ish.*, Part I, p. 365), it would be reasonable to assume that "and their like" is a part of the text.

On the basis of the explanatory phrase and the proof, one goes from what is already achieved to that which is sought. Thus there is no way to grasp an unknown object on the basis of something that is already known; furthermore, there is no way to achieve this, even given that which is already actually known, except by discerning the aspect by virtue of which the latter comes to lead to what is sought.

138 *Chapter Four. Remark: [Concerning the logician's need for knowing the principles of the explanatory phrase and the proof]*

The logician reflects on the prior principles that are appropriate for the sought objects, one by one, and on how these principles lead the inquirer to the unknown object sought. Thus the logician must do his best to know the principles of the explanatory phrase and the manner of its composition – be that in the form of a definition or otherwise; and to know the principles of proof and the manner of its composition – be that in the form of a syllogism or otherwise.

What one must first begin with are just the single elements, of which definition, syllogism and what resembles them are composed. Now let us, therefore, begin by showing how the expression signifies the concept.

139 *Chapter Five. Remark: Concerning the expression as a sign for the concept*

An expression signifies a concept [1] by correspondence – in that the expression serves as a matrix for the concept, and corresponds to it, such as "triangle" signifies "figure bounded by three sides"; [2] by way of implication – in that the concept [signified] is a part of the concept to which the expression corresponds, such as "triangle" signifies "figure" – thus, "triangle" signifies "figure" not by being a name for it but by being a name for the concept of which "figure" is a part; or [3] by way of consequence and necessity – in that the expression signifies the concept by corresponding to it, and by having this concept necessarily accompanied by another concept as an external accompaniment and not as a part of it. Rather, [this other concept] is an inseparable accompaniment of it. This is how the expression "ceiling" signifies "wall" and "human being" signifies "a being having the capacity for the art of writing." [12]

141      *Chapter Six. Remark: Concerning the predicate*

When we say that "figure" is a predicate for "triangle," this does not mean that the reality of the triangle is the same as that of the figure. Rather, what this means is that the thing which is called "triangle" is itself called "figure" – whether that thing is in itself a third concept, or one of the two.[13]

143   *Chapter Seven. Remark: Concerning single and composite expressions*

You must know that an expression may be either single or composite.

A single expression is one by the part of which, insofar as it is a part, one does not intend any signification[14] at all as, for example, when you name a person "Abd al-Lāh" (the Servant of God): for when by this you signify him as such and not his attribute of being a servant of God, you do not intend [to signify] anything at all by the word "Abd" (servant). What if you named him "Īsā" (Jesus)? Indeed, elsewhere you might say "Abd al-Lāh" and signify something by "Abd." "Abd al-Lāh" would be an attribute of him and not a [proper] name. [In such a case, "Abd al-Lāh"] is a composite and not a single expression.

A composite expression differs from a single one and it is called "a phrase." Under the latter is included a complete phrase and an incomplete phrase.

A complete phrase is one in which every part is an expression having complete signification, whether noun or verb. [The verb] is

---

[12] Signification by correspondence and signification by implication share the quality of not signifying something external to the concept, while signification by implication and signification by concomitance share the quality of requiring the signification by correspondence (*Man.*, p. 15).

[13] I.e., "figure" or "triangle."

[14] At-Ṭūsī points out that Ibn Sīnā "added to the ancient description [of a single and composite expression] the mention of 'intention' (*al-irāda*) to draw attention to the fact that the source of the signification of an expression is the speaker's intention" (*Commentary*, p. 145).

what the logicians call "a word," i.e., that which signifies an existent[15] concept of something which is undetermined in a time which is determined as one of the three times[16] [i.e., past, present, or future], for example, "rational animal." [17]

Examples of an incomplete phrase are "in the house" and "not a human being." A part of [expressions] such as these two is intended to have signification, but one of the two parts, such as "not" and "in," is a particle of which there is no full comprehension unless linked [to another term]. Thus one who says, "Zayd [is] in" or "Zayd [is] not," [18] does not fully signify what one [intends] to signify in one's example, unless one adds "in the house" or "not a human being." This is so because "in" and "not" are two particles, different from nouns and verbs.

149

*Chapter Eight. Remark: Concerning individual and universal expressions*

An expression may be either individual or universal.

---

[15] Text: *ma'nan mawjūd* (an existing concept). Our interpretation of this passage is based on a similar passage in *Naj.* (p. 11). There it reads: "The word [i.e., the verb] is a simple expression signifying a concept, and the time in which that concept exists – [that concept] being of a certain undetermined subject. An example of this is our saying, 'walked'. This signifies the walking in the past, of a walker who is undetermined."

In contrast to the verb which signifies both a concept and the time in which that concept exists, a noun signifies a concept alone. Ibn Sīnā is aware that here one may ask, "Are expressions such as 'day', 'yesterday' and 'tomorrow' words or nouns?" The answer he gives is that these are nouns. But Ibn Sīnā is also aware that one may object saying, "But a time element is involved in such expressions, something which must render them words." To this objection Ibn Sīnā responds as follows: "Not any word which signifies a time sequence is a term. For first a word should signify a meaning, and then a time element. For example, when you say 'struck', the term first refers to the verb strike, and second it refers to a period in time. But the word 'today' itself signifies a part of time. It does not first signify a meaning and then refer to a time sequence" (*Tr. Log.*, p. 20) – what Zabeeh translates here as "term," we have translated as "word."

[16] That is, the verb is an expression which gives temporal determination to the noun which is free from such determination.

[17] I.e., the complete phrase. Since the only parts of an expression that signify something by themselves are the noun and the verb, it must be the case, then, that there are two forms of a complete phrase: (1) that which consists of two nouns, such as "rational animal" – adjectives such as "rational" are considered by Ibn Sīnā as nouns; and (2) that which consists of a verb and a noun, such as, "He walks."

[18] Text: *"Zayd lā" wa "Zayd fī"* ("Zayd [is] not" and "Zayd [is] in").

CHAPTERS 8-9   53

An individual expression is such that the very conception of its essence does not permit sharing in it. An example of this is that which is conceived of [as] "Zayd."

If the individual expression is such, the universal one must then be its opposite, i.e., it is such that the very conception of its essence permits sharing in it.[19] If sharing in it is not permitted, it is due to a cause extrinsic to its comprehension.

Some universal expressions, such as "human being," are shared in actuality. Some, such as "spherical figure enclosing the twelve pentagonal sides [of a regular dodecahedron],"[20] are shared in potentiality and possibility. And some, such as "sun" according to him who believes that the existence of another sun is impossible, are not shared either in actuality, or in potentiality and possibility, due to a cause not pertaining to their very comprehension.

Examples of individual expressions are "Zayd," "this sphere enclosing them,"[21] and "this sun." Examples of universal expressions are "human being," "sphere enclosing them[22] in a non-restricted manner" and "sun."

151     *Chapter Nine. Remark: Concerning the essential,*
        *the concomitant accidental, and the separable accidental*

Among the predicates there are the essential, the concomitant accidental, and the separable accidental. Let us begin with a definition of the essential.

You must know that among the predicates there are those that are constitutive of their subjects. By "the constitutive" I do not mean the

---

[19] Compare this with Aristotle: "Some things are universal, others individual. By the term 'universal' I mean that which is of such a nature as to be predicated of many subjects, by 'individual' that which is not thus predicated. Thus 'man' is a universal, 'Callias' an individual" (*De Int.* 7, 17a, 39).

[20] Text: *al-muḥīṭ bithnataī 'ashara qā'ida mukhammasāt* (enclosing the twelve bases of pentagons). Our interpretation of this is adopted from Goichon, who notes: "le dodécaèdre régulier est la seule figure ayant pour faces douze pentagons et pouvant s'inscrire dans une sphère" (*Dir. Rem.*, p. 86, note 2).

[21] I.e., "the twelve pentagonal sides," referred to above.

[22] I.e., "the twelve pentagonal sides," referred to above.

predicate which the subject requires for the realization of its existence, such as the fact that a human being is begotten, created or made to exist, and the fact that black is an accident. I mean a predicate which the subject requires for the realization of its quiddity, and which enters its quiddity as a part of it. Examples are "figure" for "triangle," or "corporeality" for "human being." That is why, in conceiving the body as body, we can strip[23] creaturehood from [our conception of] it inasmuch as we conceive it as a body.[24] But in conceiving the triangle as triangle we cannot strip[25] figure from [our conception of] it,[26] even though this is not a common difference.[27] But there can be some non-constitutive concomitants that have this quality, as will be explained to you. But in this place there is a difference.

## Chapter Ten. Remark: Concerning the constitutive essential

You must know that everything that has a quiddity is realized either as existing in individuals or as conceived in the mind, only inasmuch as its parts are present with it. If it has a reality other than its being in existence in one of these two modes of existence, and it is not constituted by it, then existence is a concept added to its reality − [either as] a concomitant [or as] a non-concomitant.

Also the causes of its existence are other than the causes of its quiddity. Humanity, for example, is in itself a certain reality and quiddity, and its existence in individuals or in the minds is not constitutive of it[28] but is [only] added to it. / If concrete existence were

---

[23] Text: *lā yuftaqar ... ilā an namtani' 'an salb al-makhlūqiyya 'anh* (we are not in need of abstaining from negating creaturehood of it).

[24] That is, because "creaturehood" is non-constitutive of "body."

[25] Text: *wa-naftaqir ... ilā an namtani' 'an salb ash-shakliyya 'anh* (we are in need of abstaining from negating figure of it).

[26] That is, because "figure" is constitutive of "triangle."

[27] Aṭ-Ṭūsī explains this by saying, "That is, it is not a difference between the essentials and all the accidentals; for some accidentals share [this quality with the essentials], as has already been explained. Rather it is a specific difference between the essentials and the concomitants of existence which do not necessarily accompany the essence" (*Commentary*, p. 153).

[28] *Laisa annahā mawjūda fī al-a'yān aw mawjūda fī al-adhhān muqawwiman lahā.*

constitutive of it, it would have been impossible to represent the concept [of humanity] in the soul, free from that which is its constitutive part. And thus, it becomes impossible for the comprehension of humanity to be realized as existing in the soul.[29] [If, on the other hand, the existence of the quiddity in the mind is constitutive of the quiddity, then] there is doubt as to whether or not [humanity] exists concretely.[30] As for the human being, it is appropriate that there be no doubt concerning his existence, not by virtue of the comprehension of him, but by virtue of the perception of his parts. It is for you to find in other ideas an example of what we are trying to show.

Thus all the constitutives of the quiddity enter the quiddity in the concept, even though they do not come to mind separately; as many things known do not come to mind, but if they do, they are represented [in the soul]. / The essentials of a thing, according to the acknowledgement of this place in the logic, are these constitutives.

Because the primary nature[31] in which there is no difference other than in number, such as humanity, is constitutive of the particular individual coming under it, / and which the individual exceeds by his own properties [only], it is then also essential.

*Chapter Eleven. Remark: Concerning the non-constitutive concomitant accidental*

As for the non-constitutive concomitant, properly designated by the name "the concomitant," even though the constitutive is also a

---

[29] Ibn Sīnā's point here is the following: if the concrete existence is constitutive of the quiddity, then it would be impossible to represent the quiddity in the soul without its concrete existence – for you cannot eliminate any constitutive part without at the same time eliminating the quiddity. But the quiddity can be represented in the soul without its concrete existence. Hence, concrete existence is not a constitutive part of the quiddity.

[30] The text here is not clear, but it seems that Ibn Sīnā, after having shown that concrete existence is not constitutive of the quiddity, moves on to show that existence in the mind is not constitutive of the quiddity either. For if it were, then concrete existence has to include the mental one. But that is impossible, and this is why there would then be doubt concerning concrete existence. Concrete existence, however, is not in doubt. Therefore, existence in the mind is not constitutive of the quiddity.

[31] I.e., the species.

concomitant, it is that which accompanies the quiddity without being
a part of it. / An example of this is the triangle having its angles equal
to two right angles.³² This and similar concomitants necessarily
accompany the triangle in its proportions, but [only] after the triangle
is constituted by its three sides.

If [concomitants] such as these were constitutive, the triangle and
similar things would be composed of an infinite number of
constitutives. /

If the concomitance [of qualities] such as these were without an
intermediate, they would be known as having concomitance
necessarily, and thus could not be eliminated from the imagination,
even though they are non-constitutive. / [But] if they have an
intermediate which makes them evident, they would be known as
necessary through it.

By "the intermediate" I mean that which is linked to our saying,
"because it is," when it is said, "because it is such." / If this
intermediate [1] is constitutive of the thing, the concomitant is not
constitutive of [the intermediate] because the constitutive of the
constitutive is constitutive.³³ Rather it is also a concomitant of [the
intermediate.]³⁴

If the intermediate requires an intermediate, there would be an
infinite regress. Thus, it would not be an intermediate; but if it does
not require [an intermediate], it would then be a concomitant whose
concomitance is evident without an intermediate. /

If the intermediate [2] is a prior concomitant, and requires the
mediation of another concomitant, or constitutive, not leading to a

---

³² This definition of the non-constitutive concomitant together with the example given are Aristotelian. In discussing the kinds of accidents, Aristotle says, "'Accident' has also (2) another meaning, i.e., all that attaches to each thing in virtue of itself but is not in its essence, as having its angles equal to two right angles attaches to the triangle. And accidents of this sort may be eternal, but no accident of the other sort is" (*Meta.*, V, 30, 1025a, 30-34).

³³ The idea is that if the intermediate is constitutive of the quiddity, and if the concomitant of the quiddity is constitutive of the intermediate, then it follows that the concomitant is constitutive of the quiddity, because "the constitutive of the constitutive is constitutive." That is, if B is constitutive of A, and C is constitutive of B, then C is constitutive of A. But by definition, "the concomitant," as used here, is non-constitutive of the quiddity. Therefore, the concomitant cannot be constitutive of the intermediate, if the latter is constitutive of the quiddity.

³⁴ That is, as it is a concomitant of the quiddity.

concomitant without an intermediate, there will also be an infinite regress.

Thus there must be in every state, [logical or otherwise], a concomitant without an intermediate. And it has been shown[35] that this kind of concomitance cannot be eliminated from the imagination. Thus, do not pay attention to him who says that whatever is non-constitutive can be eliminated from the imagination. Among the examples of that is every number's being equal to another or unequal.

166 *Chapter Twelve. Remark: Concerning the non-concomitant accidental*

As for the predicates which are neither constitutive nor concomitant, they are all the predicates which may be separated from the subject, either in a quick or in a slow manner and either with facility or with difficulty. Examples of this are for a human being to be youthful or old, standing or sitting.[36]

167 *Chapter Thirteen. Remark: [Concerning the accidental]*

Since the constitutive is called "essential," that which is not constitutive, be it concomitant or separable, may then be called "accidental," including that which is called "an accident."[37] This we will discuss later.

168 *Chapter Fourteen. Remark: Concerning the essential in another sense*

In a place other than this in logic, "essential" may be used in another sense, i.e., to refer to the predicate which attaches to the subject due to

---

[35] See *Ish.*, Part I, p. 160.

[36] "Youthful" and "old" are examples of attributes that separate from the subject slowly; while "standing" and "sitting" are examples of attributes that separate from the subject quickly. All of these are also examples of attributes that separate from the subject with facility. As for those attributes that separate from the subject with difficulty, they are exemplified in "senility," whose separation is also slow; and in "toothache," whose separation is also quick.

[37] I.e., the common accident. But the accidental, to Ibn Sīnā, covers more than that: it covers every non-constitutive quality, i.e., property – be that concomitant, such as "the capacity of laughter" for "human being," or separable, such as "writing" for "human being"; and the common accident – be that concomitant, such as "black" for "the black human being," which he shares with "crow," or separable, such as "black" for "the desk." In other words, the accidental covers every non-essential concomitant and every separable quality.

169 the subject's substance and quiddity. / Examples of this are proportion and equality which belong to measurements or their
170 genus, / evenness and oddness which belong to number, and health and disease which belong to animal.

This sort of essentials is properly called "essential accidents." The example given of this is something like snubness for the nose.

It is [also] possible to give the essential a description combining both aspects.³⁸ /

172 That which is opposite these essentials attaches to a thing because of something external to it which is either more general than that thing, as movement attaches to a white object. For movement attaches to that object because that object is a body, and ["body"] is a more general concept than "white object." Or it is more particular
173 than [that thing], / as movement attaches to the existent. For movement attaches to it only because the existent is a body, and ["body"] is a more particular concept than "the existent"; and also as "laughter" attaches to "animal." For "laughter" attaches to "animal" only because he is a human being.³⁹

174 *Chapter Fifteen. Remark: Concerning that which is stated as the answer to the question, "What is it?"* ⁴⁰

When [the views] of the logicians who adhere to the apparent meaning are examined, they are found hardly to distinguish between the essential and that which is stated as the answer to the question "What is it?" ⁴¹ If someone of them desires to distinguish [between the two], what he says boils down to the following: that which is stated as the answer to the question, "What is it?" is that which, in spite of

---

³⁸ I.e., that which is constitutive, and that which attaches to the subject because of the subject's substance and quiddity.

³⁹ And "human being" is a more particular concept than "animal."

⁴⁰ *Al-maqūl fī jawāb mā huwa.*

⁴¹ The identity of these logicians is not made clear. But the error that Ibn Sīnā accuses them of lies in considering the genus as the answer to the question, "What is it?" when the genus, as we will soon learn, like any other essential, is a part of the quiddity which alone is stated as the answer to the question "What is it?" "Animal," which is a genus for David and Paul, cannot tell you what David and Paul are. But like "rational," it is constitutive of their nature, and is hence an element of their quiddity. Thus to the question, "What is David?" or "What is Paul?" the answer is "He is a rational animal." This is the same as saying, "He is a human being," and not "He is an animal."

175 its essentiality, is more general in the group of essentials.[42] / But then they get confused if they are shown the case of essentials that are [also] more general, [yet] without being genera, such as the things which are called "generic differences"[43] about which you will learn later.

But he who inquires about what it is, is only inquiring about the quiddity which you have already known and which is realized only through the totality of the constitutives. Thus the answer to the question "What is it?" must be given by the quiddity.

There is a difference between that which is stated as the answer to the question, "What is it?" that which enters the answer to the question, "What is it?"[44] or that which is stated on the way [to the answer] to the question, "What is it?"[45] For the answer itself is other

---

[42] I.e., the genus. In other words, the way these logicians may defend their view against the above-mentioned charge is to say that, even though, according to our view, that which is stated as the answer to the question, "What is it?" is an essential, yet it is to be differentiated from other essentials, in that it is the more general essential, since it is the genus.

[43] The above-mentioned response that these logicians may give is not acceptable to Ibn Sīnā. For, according to him, it does not succeed in distinguishing that which is stated as the answer to the question, "What is it?" from every other essential. He points out that the generic differences such as "that which is sensible" and "that which moves voluntarily" are also more general for the human individual, for example, since they are equivalent to his genus "animal." To say "that which is sensible" or "that which moves voluntarily" is to say "animal"; and to say "animal" is to say each of these expressions. But in spite of their being more general, the generic differences are not genera. Thus for these logicians, to describe that which is stated as the answer to the question, "What is it?" as the more general essential does not help them destroy the charge that they do not distinguish that which is stated as the answer to this question from every other essential.

In the following chapter we will see Ibn Sīnā dividing that which is stated as the answer to the question, "What is it?" into three types, one of them being the genus. How is this, then, to be reconciled with his vehement attack on these logicians for considering the genus as that which is stated as the answer to this question?

The genus that Ibn Sīnā refuses to accept as the answer to the question, "What is it?" is that which is a part of the quiddity, as "animal" is a part of "human being." But the genus that he considers fit to answer this question is that which is the quiddity itself, as "animal" is the quiddity of various species falling under it. In other words, it is the genus which is the common quiddity, and not that which is a part of the specific quiddity, that can tell us what a thing is.

[44] Al-dākhil fī jawāb mā huwa.

[45] Al-maqūl fī ṭarīq mā huwa.

than that which enters the answer or that which falls on the way to it.[46] /

176   You must know that, in accordance with the requirements of every language, the question of him who asks "What is it?" corresponds to "What is its essence?" or "What is the comprehension of its name?"

A thing is what it is only by virtue of the union of what it has in common with other things and what is proper to it,[47] such that its essence which is sought in this question is realized. As for the more general [essential], it is neither the identity of a thing nor the comprehension of its corresponding name.

They may say "We are using this expression[48] in another technical sense." But then they must indicate this new sense, referring [to the use of] the Ancients and pointing out [the use] they have agreed on in their transposition, as it is their custom to do.

You will soon know that it is beneficial for them to dispense with the apparent meaning of the technical language.

178   *Chapter Sixteen. Remark: Concerning the various types of that which is stated as the answer to the question, "What is it?"*

You must know that the types of [answer] which indicate what a thing is, without change in the comprehension of the technical use, are three. /

179   The first [indicates] absolute particularity, as the definition [or] name indicates the quiddity, such as "rational animal" indicates "human being." [49]

---

[46] That which is stated as the answer to the question, "What is it?" is, as we have already seen, the quiddity. As for that which enters this answer, or that which is stated on the way to this answer, it is any essential (see *Naj.*, p. 7), as "rational" or "animal" is in relation to "human being."

[47] The quiddity referred to here is the specific quiddity.

[48] I.e., that which is stated as the answer to the question, "What is it?"

[49] He who asks about what a thing is, asks about the quiddity. But if you do not answer him by the quiddity, you can answer him by the definition since "the definition is a phrase signifying the quiddity of a thing" (*Ish.*, Part I, p. 204). And since the definition differentiates the species from all others under the same genus, it is said to give "absolute particularity" in the sense that the defined is more specific than the genus.

Sometimes Ibn Sīnā also says that one can answer the question, "What is it?" by the name. That is because the name, too, corresponds to the quiddity, and is hence said

## CHAPTER 16

The second type [indicates] absolute community, as does the required answer in the question, "What is the group of different [beings] which consists of, for example, a horse, an ox, and a human being?" There, it is not necessary and not good to answer anything but "animal."[50] As for that which is more general than "animal," such as "body," it is not a common quiddity for them but is a part of a
180 common quiddity. / "Human being," "horse," and the like are, on the other hand, of a more particular signification than that which is embraced in that quiddity.[51]

If we assume that that which is sensible and that which voluntarily moves by nature share in being constitutives of and equivalent to that
181 totality,[52] still they do not indicate the quiddity. / This is so because the comprehension of "that which is sensible," "that which voluntarily moves [by nature]," and that which resembles them by way of correspondence, [indicates] a thing having the power to sense or the power to move. Similarly the comprehension of "that which is white" [indicates] a thing having whiteness. As for what those things are, that does not enter in the comprehension of these expressions except by way of concomitance, as when outside knowledge indicates that none of these things can be other than a body.

When we say, "Such an expression indicates such a thing," we are only referring by that to the manner of correspondence or implication, and not to the manner of concomitance.[53] How [could this be otherwise], when that which is indicated by way of
182 concomitance is indefinite? / Further, if that which is indicated is considered such by way of concomitance, then that which is non-constitutive could properly be said to indicate what a thing is. "That which laughs," for example, would then by way of concomitance

---

to signify it. The name "human being" signifies "human being," which is the quiddity. But the difference between the name and the definition is that while the former is a single expression, the latter is a composite one (*Man.*, p. 15).

[50] It has been said, in the last note, that the answer to the question, "What is it?" can be given either by the definition or by the quiddity. But the quiddity is either the common quiddity, i.e., the genus, or the specific quiddity, i.e., the species. This second type of answer is the common quiddity.

[51] I.e., the common quiddity.

[52] I.e., animal.

[53] For a distinction among these three manners, see Chapter 5 of the present method.

indicate "rational animal." But all had agreed that something like this is not appropriate, for what is under consideration, as the answer to the question, "What is it?" Rather it is to say of this group,[54] "They are animals." We find that the name "animal," as subject, corresponds to the totality of the common constitutives which [the members of this group] share to the exclusion of that which is proper to [every one of them]. That which is of the same character as [these common constitutives] is a general principle, free only from that which is proper to every individual of this group. /

183 As for the third type, [it indicates] both that which is common and that which is particular.[55] For example, when asked about a group consisting of Zayd, 'Amr and Khālid, "What are they?" the appropriate answer in accordance with the previously-mentioned condition is that they are human beings. And again, when asked about Zayd alone, "What is he?" – I do not say, "Who is he?"[56] – the appropriate answer in accordance with the previously-mentioned condition is that he is a human being. This is so because what is over and above humanity in Zayd are accidents and concomitants, due to causes in the matter from which he was created in his mother's

185 womb, and others which occurred to him [later on]. / It is not difficult for us to suppose that the contraries of [these accidents and concomitants] occur at the beginning of his formation; [yet] he

---

[54] I.e., the previously-mentioned group of different beings consisting of a horse, an ox, and a human being.

[55] This is the species. By "that which is common" here is meant the quiddity which the individuals of the same species share, i.e., "human being." And by "that which is particular" is meant the individual of a species taken as free from the accidents that attach to him without necessity, but taken inasmuch as some accidents such as "being one" necessarily attach to him as a result of being "human being" (*Sh. Mad.*, p. 71). Now, since the accidents that necessarily attach to the individual of a species are not constitutive elements of his quiddity, it must be the case that the species and its individuals are one in quiddity. Thus that which is particular is, in this case, identical with that which is common. That is why when you ask about one of them, "What is he?" the answer is the same, i.e., "human being." The quiddity of all human individuals is the same as that of any one of them.

[56] The question, "Who is he?" seeks what is proper to the specific individual, i.e., the accidents and not the quiddity. But the question with which the present discussion is concerned seeks the quiddity.

remains himself. But this is not how humanity is related to him, nor how animality is related to humanity and horseness.⁵⁷

This is so because the formation of the animal which is made into a human being is either completed by means of that which makes him into [a human being], in which case he becomes a human being; or it is not completed, in which case he does not become either that animal or that human being.

The previously-mentioned assumption would not be possible if [animal] were not accompanied by qualities that make him a human being,⁵⁸ but were accompanied by their contraries or / qualities other than they.⁵⁹ He would then be formed into an animal which is not a human being, such as a horse, [yet would remain] that [animal] in himself.⁶⁰ Rather, what makes him into an animal is only that which is prior to him and which makes him into a human being.

If he were [considered] under an aspect other than this, he would, then, be judged in a manner other than this. But that is not the concern of the logician.⁶¹

---

⁵⁷ That is, a human individual can be white or black, but that does not affect what he is, i.e., he remains a human being. But if you were to substitute "humanity" in him for something else, such as "horseness," he would cease to be himself. "Animality" stands to "humanity" and "horseness," as "humanity" stands to human individuals. You can substitute "humanity" in an individual animal for "horseness," yet he remains an animal. But you cannot substitute "animality" in him for something like "plantness" without changing the nature of that individual animal.

⁵⁸ I.e., "rationality."

⁵⁹ Such as "neighing," "braying," or "meowing."

⁶⁰ Which is to say that his common quiddity remains the same.

⁶¹ That is, if an individual is taken under the aspect of what is accidental, then that individual would not be considered in the same manner as any other member of his quiddity. But it is the quiddity itself and not the accidental that the logician must concern himself with.

# The Second Method

### On the Five Simple Terms,[1]
### the Definition and the Description

*Chapter One. Remark: Concerning that which is stated as the answer to the question, "What is it?" as "genus"; and that which is stated as the answer to the question, "What is it?" as "species"*

Every universal predicate, stated as the answer to the question, "What is it?" of that which falls under it, has its inferior realities either different not only numerically,[2] or different numerically only,[3] since the essentials constituting them are basically not different.[4]

The first is called "genus" with respect to that which is inferior to it and the second is called "species." It is also customary to call every one of the different realities under the first category "species" in relation to it. But when the truth is determined, the name "species" is only found to signify two different concepts in the two places.[5] / The logicians are negligent in believing that the name "species" has the same signification in the two places. Rather,[6] [its signification] differs with respect to generality and particularity.

---

[1] I.e., the five predicables.

[2] Such as "human being," "horse" and "dog." These realities differ in kind in addition to differing in number, and fall under the same genus or universal "animal."

[3] Such as John, George, and Mary. These are different only in number; their kind "human being" is the same.

[4] That is, the constitutive elements of the various individuals falling under the same species are the same. John, George and Mary are all rational animals. In contrast to that, the various realities falling under "animal," for example, have some different constitutive elements; "rational" which is constitutive of "human being" is not constitutive of "horse."

[5] I.e., where it is in itself, and where it is in relation to that which is superior to it. The former is referred to as "real species," and the latter as "relative species."

[6] Text: *aw* (or); another variation is *wa* (and).

189 *Chapter Two. Remark: Concerning the arrangement
of genus and species*

The genera may be arranged in an ascending order, and the species may be arranged in a descending order. [Each] order must be finite.[7]

As for [the questions], "With what concepts, to which 'genericity' and 'specificity' apply, does the ascending and the descending orders
190 [respectively] end?" / and "What are the intermediates between the two extremities?" they are not for the logician to determine.[8] If he makes an effort in that direction, he would be exceeding the limits of his task. Rather, he must only know that there is a summum genus or summa genera that are the genera of genera, infimae species that are the species of species, and intermediates that are genera for what is inferior to them and species for what is superior to them, and that every one of them has, in its order, [certain] characteristics.

As for investigating the quantity of the genera of genera and their quiddities to the exclusion of the intermediates and the inferior ones – as if that is important, and this is unimportant – it is going beyond what is necessary, and often inspires minds to go astray from the right path.

192 *Chapter Three. Remark: Concerning the difference*

As for the essential which is not properly stated as the answer to the question, "What is it?" of a multiplicity, in relation to which it is a universal,[9] there is no doubt that it is appropriate for making an essential distinction between this multiplicity and that which shares

---

[7] This idea and the reason for it had already been presented by Aristotle: "But it has been shown that in these substantial predications neither the ascending predicates nor the descending subjects form an infinite series; e.g., neither the series, man is biped, biped is animal, etc., nor the series predicating animal of man, man of Callias, Callias of a further subject as an element of its essential nature, is infinite. For all such substance is definable and an infinite series cannot be traversed in thought; consequently neither the ascent nor the descent is infinite since a substance whose predicates were infinite would not be definable" (*Anal. Post.* I, 22, 83b, 2-8).

[8] For these are questions of metaphysics.

[9] Text: *al-latī kulliyyatuhu* (whose universality). The pronominal suffix *-hu* must here refer to *adh-dhātī,* "the essential," which is masculine, not to *al-kathra,* "the multiplicity," which is feminine. An overly literal rendering might be "in relation to which is its universality."

193 with it existence, or a certain genus.[10] / That is why this essential is properly stated as the answer to the question, "Which thing is it?"[11] For [by the question], "Which thing is it?" one only seeks an absolute distinction between [a thing] and others sharing in its concept.[12] This [essential] is what is called "difference." /

194 This may be [1] a difference for the infima species, such as "rational" for "human being." Or [2] it may be [a difference] for the intermediate species – hence, a difference for the genus of an infima species. An example of this is "sensible" as a difference for "animal," and a difference for the genus of "human being," and not a genus for "human being" – even though it is an essential which is more general with respect to "human being."

From this it must be learned, therefore, that not every essential which is more general is a genus, nor is it stated as the answer to the question, "What is it?"[13]

Every difference is constitutive with respect to the species of which it is a difference, and divisive with respect to the genus of that species.[14]

---

[10] That is, every essential is either stated as the answer to the question, "What is it?" or it is not. The second category distinguishes a thing from other things in existence, or it distinguishes it from other things under the same genus.

An example of that which distinguishes a thing from other things in existence is "that which moves voluntarily" for "animal." This distinguishes "animal" from everything else in existence. Even though the angels and God are said to have volition and the plants are said to move; neither the angels nor God can move since they are supposed to be fully actual (for an elaboration on this point, see my Ph.D. dissertation, "An Examination of Ibn Sīnā's Solution for the Problem of Evil," p. 168), nor can the plants have volition. It remains that only animals are endowed with a voluntary movement.

An example of that which distinguishes a thing from other things under the same genus is "rational" for "human being." "Rational" distinguishes "human being" from any other being under the same genus "animal." But "rational" cannot distinguish "human being" from everything which falls outside the same genus, for the angels and God are also said to be rational.

[11] *Ay shay' huwa*.

[12] *'An al-mushārakāt fī ma'nā ash-shay'iyya*.

[13] This is a reminder that the logician's view concerning that which is stated as the answer to the question, "What is it?" mentioned earlier (pp. 175-176), namely that the answer to this question is given by the general essential, is not sound.

[14] The difference plays two roles: with respect to the species, of which it is a difference, it is an essential part; and with respect to the genus, under which this species falls, it is a dividing factor. "Rational" which is a difference for "human being" is an

196    *Chapter Four. Remark: Concerning property*
       *and the common accident*

As for property and the common accident, they are of the accidental predicates.[15]

Of the two, property is among the accidents and non-constitutive concomitants of some one universal inasmuch as it does not pertain to another – be that an infima species or a species of another type – and be it common to all [members of that universal] or not common.[16] /

197    As for the common accident, it is found in a universal and in others – be it common to all particulars or not common.[17]

---

essential part of "human being," but it distinguishes "human being" from other animal species, and hence it differentiates the genus into separate realities.

[15] Property and the common accident are therefore to be distinguished from the difference, species and genus in that while the latter three are essential, the former are accidental; but it must be remembered that all five share the quality of being universal.

[16] (1) In contrast to the difference, which is a constitutive concomitant, property is a non-constitutive concomitant. That is why it is among the accidentals.

(2) Property is a universal whose subject is also universal, be that a species or a genus. An example of a property which has a species for its subject is "the capacity to laugh" for "human being." And an example of a property which has a genus for its subject is "having three angles equal to two right angles" for "triangle" (*Naj.*, p. 17).

(3) Property in the real sense belongs to one subject only. If it can be shown, for example, that "the capacity to laugh" is not limited to "human being" but extends to all other animals, then "the capacity to laugh" would no longer be a property for "human being" but a property for "animal."

(4) Property belongs either to all the members of its subject or only to some. An example of the former is "the capacity to laugh" for "human being." This property is "concomitant and equivalent" (*Naj.*, p. 17). That is to say, the concept, "human being," is always accompanied by "the capacity to laugh," not as a constitutive part of it but as an external accompaniment which necessarily attaches to this concept after this concept had already been constituted. And its equivalent, in the sense that whenever you say, "human being," you say, "having the capacity to laugh"; and vice versa. There cannot be one human being who does not have this capacity. And an example of the latter is "peasantry" or "writing" for "human being."

[17] (1) Like property, the common accident is non-constitutive.

(2) And again like property, the common accident is a universal whose subject is also a universal.

(3) But in contrast to property, which belongs to one universal only, the common accident always belongs to more than one universal; hence its adjective is "the common."

(4) The common accident is either common to all the members of its subject or only to some (we are to understand by "common" in the expression "common

The best properties are those which are common to the species, belong to it and are inseparable concomitants of it. And the most useful ones in the identification of a thing / are those whose existence is evident. Examples of property are "the capacity to laugh" for "human being," and "equality of angles to two right angles" for "triangle." An example of the common accident is "white" for "white being."[18] Sometimes this is called "accident" without restriction, "common" being deleted from it.

The late logicians[19] believe that this accident is the accident which is the opposite of substance.[20] But this accident is not of that kind at all. Rather, the meaning of this "accident" is the accidental.[21] /

---

accident"; "shared by more than one universal"; and by "common" in the rest of the sentence, "shared by the members of the same universal").

An example of the former is "black" for "crow." "Black" in this example is a common accident applicable to all the members of the species "crow." And it is concomitant or inseparable: every crow must be black and "black" always accompanies it. Another example of a common accident which is applicable to all the members of its subject is "movement" for "animal." "Movement" in this example is a common accident for the genus "animal." And it is separable.

An example of the latter is "black" for "black human being." "Black" in this example is applicable to some members of a species. And it is concomitant. Another example is "black" for "vehicle." "Black" in the present example is applicable to some members of a genus and it is separable.

[18] *Al-bayaḍānī*: a white waterbird.

[19] I.e., Porphyry (see *Sh. Mad.*, pp. 85-87). It is passages from Porphyry such as the following that Ibn Sīnā has in mind: "What comes into being and passes away apart from the destruction of the substratum is an accident. Two types are distinguished, the separable and the inseparable. Sleeping is a separable accident, while being black occurs inseparably in the crow and in the Ethiopian" (Porphyry, *Isagoge*, pp. 48-49).

[20] Text: *al-ladhī yuqāl ma' al-jawhar* (which is stated with the substance). I am reading "*yuqābal*" (opposite) for "*yuqāl*" (stated), as it is in *Naj*. (p. 7).

[21] In *Naj*. (pp. 10-11), we are told: "As for the common accident, it is any simple universal which is accidental, that is, non-essential ... be it a substance in itself such as 'the white' (*al-abyaḍ*); or it is an accident, such as 'whiteness' (*al-bayāḍ*), which is not (Text: after not being) constitutive of the quiddity. Thus the application of 'accident' to this [i.e., common accident] and to that which is a part of the substance, in existence, is an application with two different senses" (for a similar passage, see *Naj.*, p. 7; also *Sh. Mad.*, pp. 85-87).

An analysis of this passage reveals that, according to Ibn Sīnā, a common accident is either (1) a substance, or (2) an accident, that is, a non-constitutive part of the quiddity. It is because of this double-sidedness that the common accident differs from the accident which is the opposite of the substance. For the latter is always a non-constitutive part of a substance. The common accident, on the other hand, covers but

199   A thing may be a property in relation to a universal, and a common accident in relation to that which is more particular than [that universal]. Thus "walking" and "eating" are among the properties for "animal" and among the common accidents for "human being."

200   *Chapter Five. Admonition*

These five terms, i.e., the genus, species, difference, property and the common accident, all share in being predicated, in name and in definition, of the particulars that fall under them.[22]

202   *Chapter Six. Remark: Concerning the descriptions of the five [terms]*

The genus is described as a universal predicated of things having different realities, in answer to the question, "What is it?"

The difference is described as a universal predicated of a thing, in answer to the question, "Which thing is it in its substance?"[23]

---

goes beyond the accident which is opposite the substance. Yet both are called "accident." In the present text, Ibn Sīnā wishes to draw attention to the point that, in spite of this community in name, there is the difference in meaning, indicated above.

However, it is difficult to make any sense out of this. How could any common accident be a substance, when, in the first place, the common accident is said to be non-essential? Ibn Sīnā's response is this: a common accident can be taken generally or it can be taken specifically. But whether taken generally or specifically is a relative matter. When you say, "the white human being," you are taking "the white" in a general sense; for here it can apply to many other beings, such as "snow" and "swan." As such, "the white" is, according to Ibn Sīnā, a substance because it can contain many things. But when you say, "The human being is white," you are taking "white" in a specific sense; for here it is understood to be a specific quality of "human being." As such, "white" is contained in the substance "human being" which contains many other qualities such as "height" and "weight" (*Sh. Mad.*, p. 106). Compare this with the following passage from Porphyry: "Yet, in one way accidents contain because they exist in many things, while in another they are contained because the substrata are not receptive of one accident but of many" (Porphyry, *Isagoge*, pp. 59-60).

[22] The relative species, i.e., the intermediate one which is a species in relation to that which is superior to it is not one of these predicables. For inasmuch as it is such, it is not predicated of anything. It is the real species, i.e., the infima species which is a species in itself, that counts as one of the predicables (this is made clear in the following chapter).

[23] "In its substance" is added to distinguish difference from property. For property, too, is a universal, stated as the answer to the question, "Which thing is it"? (*Naj.*, p. 10). But while difference is a constitutive element, property is not.

The species is described in one of two senses: [First, it is described] as a universal predicated of things not differing, except numerically, in answer to the question, "What is it?" [24] And in the second sense, it is described as a universal of which the genus is predicated as well as of other things, in an essential and primary manner.[25]

Property is described as a universal, stated in a non-essential manner, of that which falls under one reality only.

And the common accident is described as a universal, stated in a non-essential manner of that which falls under one reality and of others.

### Chapter Seven. Remark: Concerning definition

The definition is a phrase signifying the quiddity of a thing. And there is no doubt that it includes all the constitutives of a thing. / It is impossible for the definition not to be composed of the genus and the difference of a thing, because the common constitutives [of a thing] are its genus and [its] proper constitutive is its difference. / Unless that which is common and that which is proper unite in a composite, the composite reality of a thing is not complete. And unless a thing has a composite reality, it is not possible for an expression to signify that thing's reality. For every definable is composite in concept.

It must be known that the purpose of the definition is not to give a distinction in just any manner, nor conditioned also by being one of the essentials, without further consideration; but to give a conception of the essence, as it is.[26] /

---

[24] This is the real or infima species which is predicated of the particulars subsumed under it, and is hence one of the five predicables.

[25] This is the relative or intermediate species which is not predicated of anything, but that which is superior to it is predicated of it and of other species. By "in ... a primary manner" is meant that that which is superior to it is predicated of it without mediation, as "animal" is predicated of "human being." This is to be contrasted with "animal" as predicated of "John." The latter type of predication requires the mediation of "human being." It is because John is a human being that he is an animal.

[26] This is the Aristotelian definition of definition: "Definition is said to be the statement of a thing's nature" (*Anal. Post.*, II, Ch. 10, 29).

The definition is a statement that makes a distinction, but not just any kind of distinction. None of the accidentals that distinguish a being from some other beings in some manner are mentioned in the definition, nor is it sufficient for giving a complete definition, to mention only the difference or differences which distinguish a thing

207 If we suppose that, following its genus, a thing has two differences equivalent to it, as "animal" may be thought to have two differences such as "that which is sensible" and "that which moves voluntarily" after being a body with a soul, then when one of these two differences is mentioned alone, it is sufficient for the definition which is intended to give the essential distinction. But it is not sufficient for the definition in which one seeks the determination of the essence or reality of a thing.

If the purpose of the definition were to give a distinction by the essentials in just any manner, then our statement, "Human being is a mortal, rational body" must be a definition.

208 *Chapter Eight. Delusion and Admonition*

[Even] if the elements which one needs to mention in the definition, i.e., the constitutives of a thing, are numerous,[27] the definition cannot be given except in one manner in the expression which unites all the constitutives as arranged; and cannot be made shorter or longer. This is so because mention of the proximate genus leaves no need for enumerating the common constitutives, one by one, since the name of the genus indicates all of them implicitly. After that, [the definition] is completed by mention of the differences.[28]

[But] you have learned that if the differences are more than one, brevity and omission are not good, if the purpose of defining is to

---

essentially from other things under the same genus. One cannot define "human being," for example, by saying "He is rational." For "human being" is an animal before he is rational. "Animal," the genus, must, therefore, be mentioned in addition to "rational," the difference, in order for the definition to be complete.

Thus the definition distinguishes the concept of a thing from any other concept, by presenting it with nothing more and nothing less than it contains, i.e., its constitutives. Since the accidentals are external to the concept of a thing, they cannot be included in the definition. And since the difference is the proper constitutive of a thing and the genus the totality of its common constitutives, neither of them can be eliminated from the definition.

[27] Text: *ma'dūda* (numbered).

[28] The preceding view is the delusion of some logicians (*Naj.*, p. 79). In what follows, Ibn Sīnā tries to show that it is a mistake to assume that the definition is necessarily a brief phrase that cannot be expressed except in one form, and that this phrase cannot be abridged or prolonged. But with the other points mentioned, he has no quarrel, namely that the definition must retain the order of the constitutives and that it is completed by adding the differences to the genus.

conceive the essence of a thing as it is. [Even though] that[29] is also followed by [the essential] distinction.

If intentionally, negligently or forgetfully one substitutes the definition of the genus for its name, we would not claim that one ceases to be definer – expressing astonishment at his act of prolonging the definition.[30]

Thus neither does that kind of brevity deserve much praise, nor does that kind of prolonging deserve much blame – if the necessary union and arrangement [of constitutives] are preserved in the definition.[31] /

209 Often one benefits from an addition in the descriptions, which is over and above that which is sufficient for the distinction. You will soon learn about descriptions.

He who says that the definition is a brief phrase [stating] such and such, [refers to a phrase that] implicitly involves an explication of an unknown relative thing, because a brief phrase is indefinite. [A phrase] may be brief in relation to one thing, and long in relation to another. The use of a phrase such as the above in the definitions of non-relative things is an error they have committed in their books. This they must, therefore, remember.

210 *Chapter Nine. Remark: Concerning description*

When a thing is identified by a phrase composed of the union of that thing's accidents and properties whose totality belongs to it, then that thing is identified by its description.[32] /

---

[29] I.e., mentioning only one difference in the definition of a thing whose differences exceed one in number. Recall what was stated earlier (p. 207), that the definition which indicates the essence or reality of a thing must include all the differences. On the other hand, mention of one difference suffices for the definition whose purpose is to bring out the essential distinction only. The same idea is repeated here in order to show that while some definitions can be described as brief statements, others cannot be so described.

[30] For an elaboration on this point, see "Al-Fārābī's *Eisagoge*," ed. D. M. Dunlop, *Islamic Quarterly*, 3 (1956), 136-137.

[31] That is, if you were to say, for example, "Human being is a rational animal," or "Human being is a rational ensouled body," you would be saying the same thing. Any definition is good if the union of the proper and common constitutives is preserved, as well as the proper order of these constitutives.

[32] In a complete description, as in a complete definition, the genus must also be mentioned. If you were to mention properties and accidents without the genus, you would still have given a description but an incomplete one (*Qas. Muz.*, pp. 17-18).

## CHAPTERS 9-10

211 The best description is that in which the genus is placed first, for the purpose of determining the essence of a thing.[33] An example of this is saying of the human being, "He is an animal that walks on two feet, with broad nails and capable of laughter by nature"; and saying of the triangle, "It is a figure that has three angles." /

212 Descriptions must be of evident properties and accidents of a thing. Thus he who identifies the triangle by saying, "It is a figure whose angles are equal to two right angles," does not give a description, except for geometricians.

213 *Chapter Ten. Remark: Concerning the types of errors that occur in the identification of things by definition and description*

If [these errors] are known, they have an intrinsic benefit; and they indicate [other] forms that they have in other [identifications].

It is abominable and absurd to use metaphorical, figurative and uncouth strange expressions in definitions. Rather, the expressions

214 used in definitions must have an ordinary stipulation.[34] / If it happens that one does not find an ordinary appropriate expression for a concept, let one then coin for that concept an expression which is most appropriate, indicate that which is intended by it and then use it in [the definition]. /

215 Those who identify may be negligent in their identification.[35]

[1] For sometimes they identify a thing by that which is similar to it [in the degree of its being] known or unknown, as when one identifies the even as "a number which is not odd."

[2] Sometimes they go beyond that and identify a thing by that which is less known than it, as some say, "Fire is the element that resembles the soul." But the soul is more concealed than fire.

---

[33] That is, because the genus is the most fundamental principle of the essence. Without "animal" there can be no "human being" or "horse."

[34] For after all, every definition, like every description, is an identification of a thing which is somewhat unknown (*Man.*, p. 42). To include in it terminology which is also unknown is to defeat the purpose of the identification. You cannot make an unknown known by means of another unknown.

[35] What follows is a list of errors that are related to the concepts employed in identification. These errors are to be differentiated from the error mentioned above which is related solely to the terminology in the identification.

[3] Sometimes they go further than that, and identify a thing by itself. Thus they say, "Movement is transference," and "Human being is the human animal."

[4] And sometimes they go further than that still, and identify a thing by that which cannot be identified except by that thing, either explicitly or implicitly. Regarding the explicit case, it is exemplified in the statement, "Quality is that by means of which similitude and its opposite occur." But they cannot identify "similitude" except by [saying] that it is agreement in quality. Thus similitude is different from equality and proportion only in that it is an agreement in quality and not in quantity,[36] species or anything else. / As for the implicit case, it is such that the analysis of the identification of that by means of which a thing is identified ends with the former as being identified by that thing, even though that is not [apparent] at the beginning of [the analysis]. An example of this is when, to start with, one says, "Two is a first even number." Then one defines an even number as "That which is divisible into two equal parts." After that one defines the two equal parts as "Two things, each of which is congruent with the other."[37] And finally one defines the two things as "being two." It is impossible not to use the expression of duality in the definition of the two things, inasmuch as they are two things.

[5] Those who identify may be negligent [in another way]. Thus, they repeat a thing in the definition where there is no need or necessity for it – / I mean the necessity found in the definition of some composites and relatives, as is known from another place. An example of this error is to say, "Number is a plurality, formed of a group of units," when that which is formed of a group of units is a plurality itself. Another example is to say, "Human being is a rational corporeal animal." But "body" is included in the definition of "animal." For it is said "[Animal] is an ensouled body, sensible and moves voluntarily." Thus [one who says the above] is being repetitive. /

These two examples may be parallel to some of that which has already preceded concerning which a remark has been made – but the consideration is different.[38]

---

[36] Text: *al-kaifiyya* (quality).

[37] Text: *yuṭābiq al-ākhar mathalan* (is congruent with the other, for instance). "For instance" has been deleted, since it adds nothing.

[38] This seems to be a reference to (3). In both cases there is repetition. But while in

You must know that those who identify a thing by that which is not identified except by that thing are in the same class as those who repeat the defined in the definition.[39]

219 ## Chapter Eleven. *Delusion and Admonition*

Some people may believe that since, of two correlatives, each is known simultaneously with the other, this necessitates that each of them is known by the other, and thus each is taken in the definition of the other.[40]

[This belief is due to] the ignorance of the difference between that which [is such that] a thing cannot be known except simultaneously with it, and that which a thing cannot be known except by it. For it is impossible for that which [is such that] a thing cannot be known except simultaneously with it not to be unknown where the thing is unknown, and known where the thing is known. As for that which [is such that] a thing cannot be known except by it, it must be known before the thing [is known], and not simultaneously with it. /

220 It is abominable and absurd that a human being who does not know what a son is and what a father is and who asks, "What is a father?" is answered, "It is he who has a son." He, then, says, "Had I known what a son is, I would not have needed to inquire about what a father is, since knowledge about both is simultaneous." This is not the way [to answer this question]. Rather, a kind of a more sensitive [answer] is saying something like "A father is an animal who from his semen begets another of the same species, inasmuch as he is such." For there is nothing in any part of this explication which is explicated by "son" or which has reference to it.

---

(3) the repetition is of the defined, the repetition here is of an element already implicit in an essential part.

[39] (4), too, is in the same category as (5) and (3) in that something in it is repeated. In (4) as in (3) the defined is repeated. But the difference between the two is that while in the latter the defined is immediately thrown back at you, in the former the presentation of the defined is mediated either by one step, i.e., in the explicit case, or by a number of steps, i.e., in the implicit case.

[40] This is the delusion of some, which is another error committed in identification. But one would expect to have it listed in the previous chapter. In *Maj*. (p. 88), this error is not given a separate treatment.

Do not pay attention to what the author of the *Isagoge* says in the chapter in which he describes the genus in terms of the species.[41] This we have already discussed in *ash-Shifā'*. /

221 This is what we have wished [to show] by the remark concerning the identification of the composition leading to the concept. We will now move to identify the composition leading to the assent.[42]

---

[41] The same charge against Porphyry is made in *Maj.* (ibid.) where Porphyry is said to define the two correlatives, the genus and the species, in terms of each other. The passage from Porphyry that seems the subject of Ibn Sīnā's attack is the following: "... species is also said to be (2) that under the defined genus. We customarily say, then, that man is a species of animal, since animal is its genus; white a species of color; triangle a species of figure. In defining genus we mentioned the species by saying that the genus is predicated essentially of many things which differ in species. If we now say that the species is that under the defined genus, we ought to realize that we must define one in terms of the other since the genus is a genus of something and the species is a species of something." (Porphyry, *Isagoge*, p. 34).

[42] This marks the end of the discussion of the explanatory phrase and the beginning of the discussion of proof.

# The Third Method

### ON ASSERTIVE COMPOSITION[1]

*Chapter One. Remark: Concerning the types of propositions*

This type of composition which we have determined to mention [next] is the composition which yields an assertion, and which is one whose utterer is called "truthful" in what he says, or "a liar." / As for the utterer of something like interrogation, request, wish, aspiration, wonder, etc., he is not called "truthful" in uttering such expressions, or "a liar," i.e., inasmuch as they express an assertion.[2]

The types of assertive composition are three. /

The first is that which is called "predicative."[3] In this type, a judgment is made that an idea is predicated of another, or that it is not. Examples of this are the statements, "Human being is an animal," and "Human being is not an animal." "Human being" and the like, in what resembles this example, is what is called "subject," and that which resembles "animal" here, is what is called "predicate." As for "not," it is a negative particle.

The second and the third types are called "conditional." / A conditional proposition is composed of two assertions, each of which has been brought out of its assertive state to another. The two are then joined, not in a manner [where it could be] said that one is the other as in predicative propositions, but [either] in a manner [where it

---

[1] *At-tarkīb akh-khabarī* (informative composition). "*Khabarī*" here is the adjectival form of "*khabar*" in the sense of "proposition" (see, for example, *Naj.*, p. 12, where "*khabar*" and "*qaḍiyya*" [proposition] are used synonymously), and not in the sense of "predicate" of a grammatical subject.

[2] As when the teacher, for example, says, "Turn to page 99." While the primary function of this expression is an order, this expression nevertheless makes an assertion, as if the teacher said, "I want you to turn to page 99." This assertion is, however, secondary to this order. The same is true of interrogation, etc. But the case of assertive expressions is different: their primary function is to make an assertion (*Man.*, p. 60).

[3] *Al-ḥamlī*, i.e., the categorical proposition: "A is B," or "A is not B."

could be said] that one necessarily follows from the other or[4] attaches to it [without necessity] – this is called "connective conditional"[5] or "assumptive proposition";[6] or in a manner [where it could be said] that one is in conflict with and separate from the other – this is called "disjunctive conditional."[7]

An example of the connective conditional is the statement, "If a line falls on two parallel lines, then the exterior angle is equal to the corresponding interior one." Were it not for "if" and "then,"[8] each of the two phrases would have been an assertion by itself.

An example of the disjunctive conditional is the statement, "Either this angle is acute, or it is obtuse, or it is right." If "either" and "or" are eliminated, these phrases would be more than one proposition.

226     *Chapter Two. Remark: Concerning affirmation and negation*

A predicative affirmation is something like the statement, "Human being is an animal." The meaning of this is that the thing which we

---

[4] Text: *wa* (and). Since this type of conditional will be divided into two types (*Ish.*, Part I, p. 227) – one in which the consequent follows from the antecedent by necessity, and one in which the consequent accompanies the antecedent by chance – reading "or" instead of "and" seems more appropriate, unless a longer expression is added in brackets.

[5] *Ash-sharṭī al-muttaṣil*. This is the hypothetical proposition.

[6] *Al-waḍ'ī*.

[7] *Ash-sharṭī al-munfaṣil*. The modern reader may find it odd to name this kind of proposition "conditional." Ibn Sīnā, too, recognizes that according to the Arabic language "conditional" is the name given to the if-then statements, since these statements contain a posited condition accompanied by a response (*Man.*, p. 60). Ibn Sīnā explains why a disjunctive must be called a conditional first by explaining what a conditional is and then by showing that the disjunctive is basically a conditional. It is as if, Ibn Sīnā says, what is intended by "conditional" is any discourse consisting of more than one proposition which have lost their character of being propositions and which were turned into parts of a proposition. This is, of course, true of propositions like "If the sun is out, then it is day." "The sun is out" and "It is day" are two separate propositions. But when "if" is attached to the former and "then" to the latter, they cease being separate propositions and instead become elements of one proposition. Similarly, when you say, "Either this number is even or it is odd," you have made one proposition whose parts, "This number is even" and "It is odd," would have been separate propositions were it not for the attachment of "either" to the former and "or" to the latter (*Man.*, p. 61).

[8] *Kānat* (was). The reason for rendering *kānat* as "then" is because it represents or is the beginning of the *jawāb* (apodisis), as "*fa*" would be in some other cases. It is appropriate, therefore, to render "*kānat*" as "then."

CHAPTER 2

suppose in the mind to be a human being, be that in concrete existence or not, we must suppose to be an animal. And we judge it to be an animal without adding "when" or "in what state," but in accordance with that which is common to the temporal, the restricted and their opposites.

An example of a predicative negation is the statement, "Human being is not a stone." The state [of this negation] is the same as that [of the affirmation].[9] /

227 The connective affirmation is something like, "If the sun is out, then it is day." This is to say that if the former of the two [assertions], i.e., that to which the conditional particle is linked and which is called "the antecedent," is assumed realized, then the latter to which the particle introducing the response is linked,[10] and which is called "the consequent," necessarily follows it or accompanies it without the addition of something else.[11]

The connective negation is that which negates this necessary consequence or accompaniment. An example of that is the statement, "It is not the case that if the sun is out, then it is night."

The disjunctive affirmation is exemplified in the statement, "Either this number is even, or it is odd." This is what necessitates the disjunction and conflict.

And the disjunctive negation is that which negates the disjunction and conflict. An example of this is the statement, "It is not the case that either this number is even, or it is divisible into two equal parts."

---

[9] That is, it is applicable to both the external existent, the temporal and the restricted on the one hand, and to the non-external existent, the non-temporal and the non-restricted on the other. In other words, pure affirmation as well as pure negation hold true whether their object has external existence or not, and whether it is in time or conditioned in another manner or not.

[10] *Ḥarf al-jazāʾ*, also called *"al-rābiṭa li-jawāb ash-sharṭ"* (the particle linking the answer to the condition: the particle connecting the consequent and the antecedent).

[11] I.e., without necessity. In a connective conditional, the consequent is linked to the antecedent either by necessity or by chance. "If the sun is out, then it is day" is an example of the former since it cannot fail to be true that, whenever the sun is out, it is day. "If it is night, then my bird is asleep" is an example of the latter since there is no necessary link between its being night and a bird's sleep. A bird may be awake at night, and asleep during the day (see aṭ-Ṭūsī, *Commentary*, p. 227).

### Chapter Three. Remark: Concerning singularity, indefiniteness[12] and definiteness[13]

If a proposition is predicative, and its subject is a particular thing, it is called "singular" whether affirmative or negative. Examples of this are, "Zayd is a writer," and "Zayd is not a writer."

If the subject of a predicative proposition is universal but the quantity – I mean, the universality or particularity – of the judgment is not revealed but is indefinite such that there is no indication concerning whether or not it is common to all that which is subsumed under the subject, the proposition is called "indefinite." Examples of this are, "Human being is at loss," and "Human being is not at loss."

If the introduction of "al" (the) necessitates generality and community, and the introduction of "at-tanwīn" (nunnation) necessitates particularity, then there is no indefinite proposition in the Arabic language[14] and must be searched for in another language. As for [the determination of] the truth of this matter, it is left for the discipline of grammar, which we do not confuse with other disciplines. If the subject of a predicative proposition is universal and the extension of the judgment concerning it and the quantity of the subject are revealed, then the proposition is called "definite." / If it is evident that the judgment is general, the proposition is called "universal." This is either affirmative, such as "Every human being is an animal," or it is negative, such as "No human being is a stone." If it is evident that the judgment is about some and does not extend to the rest, or that it extends [to the rest] in an indirect manner, then the definite proposition is "particular." It is either affirmative, such as "Some human beings are writers," or negative, such as "Some human beings are not writers," or "Every human being is not a writer." The meaning of the [last] two propositions is one. They are not general in negation. /

---

[12] *Al-ihmāl*: literally, negligence, i.e., negligence of the determination of the quantity of the judgment.

[13] *Al-ḥaṣar*: literally, limitation, a reference to the determination of the quantity of the judgment.

[14] In the Arabic language, one of the uses of *al*, as Ibn Sīnā will point out soon, is three-fold, one of which is to indicate universality. Nunnation, on the other hand, indicates particularity. Hence, if the above-mentioned use were the only one that *al* has, there would be no room for indefinite expression in the Arabic language.

231   You must know that even though in the Arabic language one may indicate generality by "the," one may also indicate by it the determination of a nature.[15] And there the place of "the" is not the same as that of "every." Do you not see that you say, "The human being[16] is common, and is a species," and you do not say, "Every human being is common, and is a species?" Again, you say, "The human being is a laughing creature," and you do not say, "Every human being is a laughing creature." "The" may also be used to indicate a particular thing that has already been mentioned, or whose state has already been known. Thus you say, "the man," by which you mean a specific individual. A proposition [having such a particular thing as a subject] is, then, singular.[17] /

232   You must know that the word that determines the quantity is called "quantity indicator."[18] Examples are "every," "some," "none," "not every," "not some," and that which resembles them, such as "the whole" and "everybody" in the affirmative universal, and such as "*hīch*" (nothing) in Persian, in the negative universal.

233      *Chapter Four. Remark: Concerning the judgment*
            *of the indefinite proposition*

You must know that the indefinite proposition does not necessitate generalization. This is because in it there is mention of a nature which can be either properly taken universally or properly taken particularly. Taking it purely [i.e., by itself], without linkage [to a quantity indicator] does not necessarily make it universal. If that were necessarily to impose universality and generality on it, then the nature of "human being" would have necessarily been general – and

---

[15] "Nature" is used here in the sense of "essence" or "quiddity."

[16] In English it is more appropriate to say, "Human being is common, and is a species." But since Ibn Sīnā's purpose here is to point out the different uses of "the" in the Arabic language, the statement was left in its Arabic form. The same procedure is followed in the first statement of the following example.

[17] Thus, "the" is used in Arabic in three senses: (1) as a universal quantifier; (2) as an indicator of indefiniteness when the purpose is to refer to a nature without any reference to the quantity; and (3) as a demonstrative pronoun, to refer to something that has already been mentioned, or to something that is already known, thus rendering the proposition singular.

[18] *Sūran*: literally, fence, or that which draws a limit.

thus an individual would not be a human being. But since it can be properly taken universally, and there, it can also be applicable particularly; for that which is predicated of all is predicated of some – the same being true of [that which is predicated] negatively – and [since] it can be properly taken particularly, then in the two cases its judgment is applicable particularly. Thus the indefinite proposition is of the same force as that of the particular one.

But the fact that a proposition is explicitly applicable particularly does not prevent it from being at the same time applicable universally. / For if a judgment is made about some, it does not follow from this that the rest is the opposite. Thus even though the indefinite proposition is explicitly of the same force as a particular one, there is nothing to prevent it from being applicable universally.

### Chapter Five. Remark: Concerning the definiteness and indefiniteness of conditional propositions

In conditional propositions, there may also be indefiniteness and definiteness. Thus if you say "Whenever the sun is out, then it is day," or "Always this number is even, or it is odd," then you have given affirmative universal definiteness. And if you say "It is never the case that if the sun is out, then it is night," or "It is never the case that either the sun is out, or it is day," then you have given negative universal definiteness.

If you say "Sometimes, when the sun is out, the sky is cloudy," or "Sometimes, Zayd is in the house, or 'Amr is in the house," then you have given affirmative particular definiteness.[19] And if you say, "It is not the case that whenever the sun is out, then the sky is cloudy;" or "It is always the case that either fever is choleric,[20] or it is inflammatory,"[21] then you have given negative particular definiteness.

---

[19] In Dunyā's edition, the text for this chapter ends here. But in Forget's edition, the text goes on to give two examples of definite negative particular conditionals. We have accepted Forget's version since this would complete the list of examples of the four types of definite conditionals: affirmative universal, negative universal, affirmative particular and negative particular.

[20] *Ṣafrāwiyya*.

[21] *Damawiyya*.

238     *Chapter Six. Remark: Concerning the composition*
*of conditional propositions from predicative ones*

You must know that all conditional propositions are analyzed into predicative ones, and are not directly analyzed into simple parts. As for the predicative propositions, they are those that are directly analyzed into simple parts, or into that which is of the same force as the simple.[22]

The two parts of the predicative propositions are either simple, such as in the statement, "The human being walks," or of the same force as the simple, such as in the statement "The mortal rational animal walks," or "[He] moves by moving his two feet." This is only of the same force as the simple, because what is intended here is one thing in its essence, or one concept, which can be signified by one word.

239     *Chapter Seven. Remark: Concerning equipollence*[23]
*and positiveness*[24]

Sometimes the composition consists of a negative particle with another [term], as in the statement, "Zayd is non-sighted." By "non-sighted" we intend "blind," or a concept more general than that.[25] /
240    In short, if "non" is made as one thing with "sighted," or with what resembles it, and is, then, affirmed or negated, "non" – as well as any other negative particle [in its place] – is, then, a part of the predicate. Thus if you affirm the whole, that would be an affirmation.

---

[22] The parts of the proposition are the subject and the predicate. A subject or a predicate is simple when it does not signify more than one concept, such as "human being" or "walks." And what is of the same force as the simple is the complex expression but which refers to one concept and can be replaced by a simple expression, such as "the mortal rational animal" or "walks on two feet."

[23] *Al-'udūl*. An equipollent proposition is one in which either the subject, the predicate, or both are composed of a simple positive expression and a negative particle (for what a positive expression is, see the following note).

[24] *At-taḥṣīl*. By "positive" is meant "real," in the sense of "existent." But the term is extended to mean any affirmative simple expression. Thus "blind" which indicates a privation of being is taken to be a positive expression.

[25] I.e., by "non-sighted" is intended the lack of sight in a being whose nature is to have sight, or the lack of sight whether in a being whose nature is to have sight or in a being whose nature is not to have sight.

And if you negate it, that would be a negation, as when you say, "Zayd is not non-sighted."

It must be known that every predicative proposition must have, in addition to the idea of the subject and that of the predicate, an idea of the union between the two. This is a third idea in addition to the other two. / If one presumes that words correspond to ideas in number, then this third [idea] must have a third word signifying it.

In some languages this word may be omitted, as is the case at times in the original Arabic language. An example of this is the statement, "*Zayd kātib*" (Zayd a writer), when it must be said, "*Zayd huwa kātib*" (Zayd is a writer). But in some languages this word cannot be omitted. For example, in original Persian, "*ast*" (is) [cannot be omitted] from the statement, "*Zayd dabīrast*" (Zayd is a writer). This word is called "copula."[26] /

[In Arabic], if a negative particle precedes the copula, as in the statement, "*Zayd laisa huwa baṣīran*" (Zayd is not sighted), then negation has been applied to the affirmation, thus eliminating it and negating it. But if the copula precedes the negative particle, it makes it a part of the predicate.[27] And the proposition is an affirmation as in the statement, "*Zayd huwa ghayr baṣīr*" (Zayd is non-sighted).

---

[26] *Rābiṭa*: literally, linking particle.

[27] In some other languages such as in English, the negative particle applies to the copula, not by preceding but by following it. Thus in English we say, "Human being is not a stone," and not "Human being not is a stone." In Arabic, on the other hand, if the negative particle is to negate the copula, it has to precede it. But if the copula were to precede the negative particle, then the copula is not negated, and the negative particle is made a part of the predicate. Thus in Arabic the place of the negative particle with respect to the copula is what helps us distinguish between a negative particle which applies to the copula, and hence negates the subject-predicate relation, and one which is a part of the predicate.

This is so with regard to tripartite propositions, i.e., propositions that have a subject, a predicate and a copula. But as we have learned, in Arabic the copula is sometimes suppressed. Propositions with a suppressed copula are the bipartite propositions. Now the question is, how can we distinguish in bipartite propositions the negative particle which negates the subject-predicate relation from that which is a part of the predicate? Ibn Sīnā's answer is that such a distinction can be made, first, based on the intention of the speaker, and second, based on convention.

Regarding the first point, Ibn Sīnā tells us that if one says, "*Zayd lā baṣīr*," and intends by it, "*Zayd lais huwa baṣīr*" (zayd is not sighted), then this is a negation; but if one intends by it, "*Zayd huwa lā baṣīr*" (Zayd is not-sighted), then this is an affirmative equipollent proposition.

## CHAPTER 7

Sometimes [the negation] is doubled, as in the statement "*Zayd lais huwa ghayr baṣīr*" (Zayd is not non-sighted). The former [negative particle] precedes the copula for the purpose of negation, and the latter is preceded by the copula which renders it a part of the predicate. A proposition whose predicate is such is called "equipollent," "altered" and "non-positive."[28] / This may also be recognized with regard to the subject.[29]

The equipollent [expression] either indicates the privation which is opposite the possession or another [lack] such that "non-sighted" indicates "blind" only, or "any animal deprived of sight – whether [sight] belongs to its nature,[30] or to something more general than that."[31] It is not for the logician to show that this is so, but for the

---

Regarding the second point, it has become customary to use some negative particles such as "*lais*" for the purpose of negation, and "*ghayr*" for the purpose of equipollence (*Naj.*, p. 16).

But first, how are we to know the speaker's intention? The point concerning convention gives a better ground for making the distinction. But it too suffers from some difficulty. For there are some negative particles that are used for the purpose of negation as well as that of equipollence. "*La*" is one such example, as the above-mentioned passage shows.

[28] *Ma'dūla, wa-mutaghayyira, wa-ghayr muḥaṣṣala*. Each of these three names depicts one aspect of this type of proposition. "Equipollent" is a reference to its being equal in affirmation to a proposition whose terms are simple and positive. "Altered" is a reference to its having been transformed from the original state of having positive terms to having a negative particle attach to at least one of its terms, as a part of that term. And "non-positive" is a reference to its being the contrary of a proposition whose terms are positive.

[29] That is to say, a proposition is equipollent either when its predicate is an equipollent expression or when its subject is such. An example of the latter is "Non-celestial beings are mortal." A proposition whose predicate is equipollent is, according to Ibn Sīnā, of absolute equipollence (*Naj.*, p. 15); and a proposition whose subject is such is of restricted equipollence. Ibn Sīnā's concern is more with the absolute equipollent proposition than with the restricted type. This is because he wishes to make clear the various differences between an absolute equipollent proposition and a simple negative one, in order to prevent confusion between the two. But the restricted equipollent proposition is not in danger of being a part of this confusion.

[30] I.e., specific or generic nature.

[31] I.e., whether sight belongs to its species, its genus or to something more general (*Naj.*, p. 16). Ibn Sīnā's purpose here is to draw a distinction between an equipollent proposition and a privative proposition. While the former indicates any kind of lack, the latter indicates only the privation of what belongs to the nature of a thing, be that specific or generic. Take, for example, the following statements: "Zayd is non-sighted,"

244 linguist [who must investigate this matter] with respect to every language. / The logician must only assume that if the negative particle comes after the copula, or is governed by it in any manner, then the proposition is an affirmation, be it true or false; and that it is impossible for the affirmation to apply, except to something positive, represented either in [external] existence or in the mind.[32] Thus a judgment can be affirmed of a thing in accordance with that thing's
245 positive character. / As for negation, it can also properly be made of a non-positive object whether or not its non-positiveness is necessary.[33]

246 *Chapter Eight. Remark: Concerning conditional propositions*

You must know that connective and disjunctive conditionals may be composed of conditional propositions, predicative ones or a mixture [of both]. /
248 Thus, if you say, "If, whenever the sun is out, it is day, then either the sun is out, or it is not day," you have formed a connective conditional, composed of a connective conditional and a disjunctive one. If you say, "Either if the sun is out, then it is day; or not if the sun is out, then it is not night," you have formed a disjunctive conditional, composed of two connective conditionals. And if you say, "If this is a number, then either it is even or it is odd," you have formed a connective conditional, composed of a predicative proposi-

---

"the mole is non-sighted," and "the stone is non-sighted." While every one of these statements is equipollent, it is only the first two that are privative.

[32] *Wahm*. This has been translated here as "mind" and not as "imagination," because mythical figures such as the phoenix which are represented in imagination are excluded by Ibn Sīnā from being objects to which affirmation applies (ibid.).

[33] Let us summarize the differences between a simple-negative proposition and an equipollent one.

(1) In the former, a negative particle negates the subject-predicate relation, while in the latter, a negative particle is a part of the subject, the predicate or both.

(2) The former is more general than the latter, due to the fact that a negation is applicable to an existing as well as to a non-existing subject; while an affirmation, whether in an equipollent proposition or in a positive one, is not applicable except to an existing subject – regardless of whether it is the nature of the subject to have that predicate or not. Thus we are told, "It is appropriate to say that the phoenix is not sighted, but it is not appropriate to say that the phoenix is non-sighted" (ibid.).

tion and a disjunctive one. It is for you to enumerate the remaining divisions.[34] /

250 Of disjunctive conditionals, there are:

[1] The real disjunctive.[35] This is the disjunctive in which "or" is intended [to indicate] that it is impossible for the thing not to have one of the two parts [of the conditional]. Yet it must have one of them 251 only. The disjunction may consist of two parts / or of more, and it may be of an indefinite quantity.

[2] There is also the unreal disjunctive.[36] [A] This is the disjunctive in which "or" is intended [to indicate] the idea that only the union of the parts is prevented, but that the exclusion [of all] of them is not prevented. For example, when one says "This thing is an animal and a tree," you answer, "Either it is an animal, or it is a tree." The same 252 is true of all similar examples. / Or

[B] Of disjunctives, there is that in which "or" is intended to prevent the exclusion [of all parts], yet allow their union. This is [the disjunctive] whose analysis leads to the elimination of a part of the real disjunction, and the mentioning of its consequence, if it is not equal to it, but more general than it.[37] An example of this is the statement, "Either Zayd is in the sea, or he is not drowned." That is, "... or he is not in the sea," from which it follows that he is not drowned.[38]

---

[34] I.e., types of conditionals composed of various combinations of the three types of propositions: predicative, connective conditional and disjunctive conditional.

[35] *Al-ḥaqīqiyya*. This is the disjunctive which is true when one and only one of its parts is true. Otherwise it is false.

[36] *Ghayr ḥaqīqiyya*. This disjunctive is of two types, as the text will show: (A) where both parts can be false, but not both parts can be true; and (B) where both parts can be true, but not both parts can be false.

[37] In other words, if you have a real disjunctive, such as "Either it is day, or it is night," you can take "it is night," for example, and replace is by what follows from it and is more general than it, namely, "it is dark." Thus it becomes possible for you to retain both parts of the disjunctive – for it is possible that it is day, and that there is a solar eclipse which darkens the earth – but impossible not to have at least one part of the disjunctive; for it cannot fail that it is either day or it is dark. That is what is meant by saying that the exclusion is prevented.

[38] "Either Zayd is in the sea, or he is not in the sea" is a real disjunctive. "... he is not in the sea" has been replaced by its consequence which is at the same time more general than it: "... he is not drowned." From the fact that one is not in the sea, it

88   THE THIRD METHOD

The first example[39] is one in which what is possible only with the contradictory is mentioned, and not what is a consequence of the contradictory. In this the union [of the parts] is prevented, but not [their] exclusion. [The second example] [40] prevents the exclusion, but does not prevent the union. / Of the unreal disjunctive, there may be other types. But what has been mentioned here is sufficient.

In definiteness, indefiniteness, contradiction and conversion, you must treat the connective and disjunctive conditionals as you would treat predicative ones, with the antecedent as a subject and the consequent as a predicate.

### Chapter Nine. Remark: Concerning the dispositions that accompany propositions, and that give them specific judgments in definiteness and in other cases

The expression "only" [41] may be added in predicative propositions. Thus one says, "Only human being is an animal;" and "Only some human beings are writers." This addition of "only" is accompanied by an addition in the meaning not required before this addition, i.e., by the mere predication. For this addition makes the predication equal to or proper to the subject.

Similarly, you may say, "Human being is the laughing creature" – with "the" in the Arabic language, [i.e., as preceding the predicate] – thus indicating that the predicate is equal to the subject.

Again, you say "It is not the case that only human being is an animal," or "It is not the case that human being is the laughing creature," by which you indicate the negation of what was indicated in the former two affirmations. /

---

follows that one cannot be drowned; but not being drowned is a broader concept than not being in the sea, for you can be in the sea and yet not drown. Thus, we get "Either Zayd is in the sea, or he is not drowned," which is a disjunctive of the type (2B). For the union of the two parts is possible: as mentioned, he can be in the sea and not drown; but it is impossible for him not to be either in the sea or not drown. And thus the exclusion of all parts is prevented.

[39] I.e., "Either this is a tree, or it is an animal."
[40] "Either Zayd is in the sea, or he is not drowned."
[41] *Innamā* (only, merely, just or except).

256     You also say, "Human being is not, except[42] a rational creature." This may be understood in one of two senses. The first is that the meaning of "human being" is nothing but the meaning of "rational," and that "humanity" does not require any other meaning. And the second is that there is no human being who is not rational; rather, every human being is rational.

In conditional propositions, you also say, "When it is a bright day, then the sun is out." This requires, with the affirmative connection, an indication that the antecedent is admitted and posited in order to give way for the positing of the consequent.

In a like manner you say, "It is not day, except if the sun is out," by which you mean that whenever it is day, then the sun is out. And this statement gives definiteness to the meaning.

You also say, "It is not day, or the sun is out." This is close [in meaning] to that.[43] /

257     And you also say, "This number does not have an even square, when it is odd." This is of the same force as the statement, "Either this number does not have an even square, or it is not odd."

258     *Chapter Ten. Remark: Concerning the conditions of propositions*

In the predicative, connective and disjunctive propositions, you must pay attention to the condition of relation. For instance, if one says, "C is a father," attention must be paid as to whose [father he is]. Similarly, [you must pay attention to] the time, place and condition. For example, if one says, "Every movable changes," attention must then be paid [to the fact that this is so] as long as it moves. Again, attention must be paid to the condition of the part and the whole and to the condition of potentiality and actuality. Thus if one says "Wine is intoxicating," attention must be paid as to whether this is so in
259 potentiality or in actuality and in a small part / or in a large quantity.

Negligence of such ideas leads to much error.

---

[42] *Illā*.
[43] I.e., to the last example given.

# The Fourth Method

THE MATTERS AND MODES OF PROPOSITIONS[1]

*Chapter One. Remark: Concerning the matters of propositions*

In a proposition, whether affirmative or negative, the predicate and what resembles it[2] cannot fail / to have [one of three] relations to the subject:

[1] a relation of that whose existence is necessary in the thing itself[3] such as "animal" in the statements, "Human being is an animal;" or "Human being is not an animal;"

[2] a relation of that whose existence and non-existence are not necessary, such as "writer" in the statements, "Human being is a writer;" or "Human being is not a writer;" or

[3] a relation of that whose non-existence is necessary, such as "stone" in the statements "Human being is a stone," or "Human being is not a stone."

---

[1] "Matter of a proposition" is used in two senses: (1) to refer to the subject or antecedent and the predicate or consequent of a proposition; or (2) to refer to the relation between the two. It is in the latter sense that Ibn Sīnā is using the expression here. This relation can be either (1) in a manner which cannot be otherwise (necessity of existence); (2) can be otherwise (possibility); or (3) cannot but be otherwise (impossibility; necessity of non-existence) – (1) and (3) are subsumed under necessity.

But "necessity," "possibility" and "impossibility" are also referred to as "modes." So what is the difference between the matter and the mode of a proposition? Here is Ibn Sīnā's answer:

"The difference between the mode and the matter [of a proposition] is that the mode is an explicit expression signifying one of these ideas [i.e., necessity, possibility or impossibility]; while the matter is the state of the proposition in itself [i.e., in reality], not made explicit. The mode and the matter may be different, as in 'It is possible that Zayd is an animal.' The matter [in this] is necessary, while the mode is possible. There are other differences between the two which we need not develop" (*Naj.*, p. 18).

[2] I.e., the consequent of a conditional proposition.

[3] I.e., in reality.

All the matters of propositions are, then, these: [1] a matter necessary in existence,[4] [2] a possible matter, and [3] an impossible matter.

By "matter" we mean the three states of which these three expressions are, if used explicitly, true in affirmation.

263  *Chapter Two. Remark: Concerning the modes of propositions, and the difference between an absolute and a necessary proposition*

Every proposition, either:

[1] is absolute, with common application.[5] This is the type of proposition in which a judgment is presented, without mention of its necessity, duration, or anything else concerning its being in time, or
264  in accordance with possibility.[6] / Or

[2] it is a proposition in which something of that is mentioned: either necessity, duration without necessity, or existence without duration or necessity.[7]

---

[4] *Wājiba.* This is to be distinguished from "*ḍarūriyya*" (necessary). The former refers to the necessary in existence while the latter refers to the necessary in general, whether in existence or in non-existence (the impossible). In other words, both the necessary in existence and the impossible are particular cases of *ḍarūriyya* (ibid., p. 20). Thus even though "*wājiba*" and "*ḍarūriyya*" are both necessary, it must be remembered that they are such in different senses. Some have translated both as "necessary," without attention to the distinction (see, for example, Goichon, *Dir. Rem.*, p. 134). But in order to preserve this important distinction the former has been translated here as "necessary in existence" and the latter as "necessary."

[5] This is the non-modal proposition. It is absolute in the sense that it is free from modality, and it is said to have common application, i.e., to all modal propositions. This is so because it is nothing but a pure affirmation or a pure negation which is the basic character of every proposition.

[6] These are the four modes mentioned by Ibn Sīnā: (1) Necessity, which is duration. (2) Duration: this is a more general mode than necessity; necessity is duration, but duration can be free from necessity (see pp. 269-270, 278 of the present method) – a thing may endure, not by necessity but by chance (aṭ-Ṭūsī, *Commentary*, p. 264). (3) Temporality: this is to be distinguished from (1), in that it may be necessary (in a restricted manner, to be elaborated later in this chapter) without duration; and it is to be distinguished from (2), in that it may endure (in a restricted manner, perhaps for a second) without necessity. And (4) possibility.

[7] These are the first three modes in the order, indicated in the last note. But (4) is missing.

Necessity may be either [1] absolute, as in the statement, "God, exalted, exists;"⁸ / or [2] linked to a condition.

A condition may be either: [A] The duration of the existence of the essence, as in the statement, "Human being is necessarily a rational body." By this we do not mean that human being has not ceased, and will not cease to be a rational body; for this is false of every human individual. Rather, we mean by this that as long as his essence as human exists, he is a rational body. The case is the same in every negation resembling this affirmation.⁹

[B] The duration of the subject's being qualified by that [quality] which is made to accompany it, as in the statement, "Every movable changes." This does not mean absolutely or as long as its essence exists but as long as the essence of the movable moves. / There is a difference between this condition and the first one. For the first condition involves a fundamental essence, i.e., human being, while the present condition involves an essence accompanied by a quality, i.e., the movable. For the movable has an essence and a substance to which movement¹⁰ and the lack of movement¹¹ can attach. Neither human being nor black is such.¹²

[C] The condition [of the duration of the existence] of the predicate.¹³

---

⁸ This is the necessity that ties the predicate to the subject eternally. The predicate has never ceased and will never cease to belong to the subject. This necessity is absolute in the sense that it is free from linkage to a condition. Its other name is "eternal necessity." Eternal necessity is considered by Ibn Sīnā as real, but the first type of conditioned necessity, soon to be discussed, is also real according to him. It must be remembered that by "necessity" is meant both "necessity of existence" as well as "necessity of non-existence." An example of eternal necessity of existence has been given. The following is an example of eternal necessity of non-existence: "God is originated" – taking "God" in Ibn Sīnā's sense, i.e., eternal etc.

⁹ That is, in every negative proposition which is necessary, such as "Human being is necessarily not a stone." The necessity here holds as long as the essence of the subject remains human.

¹⁰ Text: *al-mutaḥarrik* (the movable).

¹¹ Text: *al-mutaḥarrik* (the movable).

¹² I.e., is such an essence which is accompanied by a quality. For "human being" is a pure essence, free from attachment to any qualities; and "black" is not an essence of any sort but a mere quality.

¹³ Necessity in this sense endures as long as the predicate belongs to the subject in existence; and without that, there is no necessity. An example of this is "Zayd is by necessity walking, i.e., as long as he walks;" for it is possible for him not to be walking when he walks (*Naj.*, p. 21).

[D] [The condition of] a non-determined time, such as that of respiration. /

267  Even though necessity, conditioned in the first manner, falls in a type different from that of absolute necessity in which there is no consideration of a condition, nevertheless it also shares with it the idea of a community of the more general and the more particular;[14] or of a community of two more particulars subsumed under a more general – if it is a condition of the conditioned proposition that the essence does not have a permanent existence – what they share is what is intended by the expression "necessary proposition." [15] /

268  As for the remaining [types of propositions] which involve the condition of necessity, and those which endure without necessity,
269  they are the types of non-necessary absolute propositions.[16] / An

---

[14] The first type of conditioned necessity is of two kinds. Either (1) it is a condition of this necessity that the essence of the subject exists always – where the essence has permanent existence; or (2) it is a condition of it that the essence of the subject exists for a certain period – where the essence is corruptible.

Absolutely necessity is one in which the essence of the subject has permanent existence. Now if attention is paid to this fact, without attention to whether this is so unconditionally or conditionally, then absolute necessity becomes the same sort as (1) of the first type of conditioned necessity. From this, it is clear that by "the more general" is intended the first type of conditioned necessity, since it includes but goes beyond absolute necessity. And by "the more particular" is intended absolute necessity, since it is a particular case of the first type of conditioned necessity (a compressed passage of *Naj.*, p. 20 gave us the clue to the interpretation of this point).

[15] If, on the other hand, attention is paid to (2) of the first type of conditioned necessity, without attention to (1) of the same sort of necessity, then the first type of conditioned necessity is no longer one under which absolute necessity is subsumed. Rather, both become particular cases of necessity in the general sense – general to the types of real necessity.

[16] Non-necessary propositions are of two types: (1) those that endure without necessity; and (2) those necessary propositions whose necessity is conditioned in the last four manners indicated above, i.e., 2B-2E – these propositions are necessary, but their necessity does not endure. The types of propositions whose necessity is conditioned in these manners are non-necessary in the sense of "not necessary in a real sense." And when they are classified under "necessary propositions," it is because they are necessary in an unreal sense (*Man.*, pp. 68, 79). The distinction between real and unreal necessity must be kept in mind if any sense is to be made of Ibn Sīnā's discussion of necessity.

Now, the puzzle is, why does Ibn Sīnā refer to these propositions as "absolute"? We know that the expression "absolute proposition" has been used by Ibn Sīnā in the sense of "non-modal." The present use is certainly not that, for non-modal propositions are free, among other things, from necessity without duration and duration without

example of that which endures and is non-necessary is something like the affirmation or negation, applicable to an individual, [of a quality] accompanying him in a non-necessary manner as long as he exists; as you may correctly say that some human beings have white complexions as long as their essence exists, even though that is not necessary.

He who believes that non-necessary predication is found in universal propositions has committed an error. For it is possible that universal propositions have that which is applicable, affirmatively or negatively, to every individual subsumed under them – if they have a multiplicity of individuals – at a determined time as that of the rising and the setting of the stars and that of the eclipse of the sun and the moon; or at an undetermined time as that which belongs to every born human being such as respiration or that which resembles it. /

Propositions which involve necessity as conditioned by something other than [the existence of] the essence may properly be called "absolute," and may properly be called "concrete," [17] as we have

---

necessity, which belong to these propositions. These propositions are called "absolute" in the sense that they are free from the condition of pure possibility, pure in the sense that it is a mere potentiality, and the condition of real necessity: they are neither non-existent nor existent in a real necessary manner (*Naj.*, p. 21; *Man.*, p. 78). In this reference from *Naj.*, these propositions are called "absolute" in that they are free from conditions; but we are not told what these conditions are. In *Man.* these conditions are said to be that of possibility and that of necessity. Propositions that are absolute in this sense are modal, because, as Ibn Sīnā puts it, their freedom from possibility and necessity is a judgment (*Man.*, p. 78), added to the pure affirmation or negation of a proposition which is absolute, with common application.

[17] *Al-wujūdiyya*, literally, existential. This name of these propositions emphasizes the fact of their existence, the fact that they are no longer in pure possibility but have attained a certain degree of necessary existence. This name is not in opposition to their other name "absolute" but points out an aspect of them other than that pointed out by the latter. As mentioned, "absolute" tells us that they are neither of pure possibility nor necessary in a real sense, and says nothing about their existence. "Concrete," on the other hand, tells us that they now exist – their possibility has necessarily been transformed into existence; and says nothing about their not having pure possibility or real necessity. These propositions are about concrete objects of this world, objects in time and space. That is why we found it appropriate to translate "*al-wujūdiyya*" as "concrete." Translating it as "contingent" is inappropriate because the first type of conditioned necessity, which is not one of these propositions, can also be said to be contingent since necessity there depends upon the duration of the existence of the essence.

reserved [the latter name] exclusively for them even though there is no quibble over names.

272    *Chapter Three. Remark: Concerning the mode of possibility*

By "possibility" is meant either:

[1] That which accompanies the negation of the necessity of non-existence – [the necessity of non-existence] being the impossibility attributed to a subject. There, in accordance with this first sense, that which is not possible is, then, impossible. "Possibility," in this sense, is predicated of the necessary in existence.[18]

[2] By "possibility," in accordance with the proper sense that has been handed down to us, is meant that which accompanies the negation of both the necessity of non-existence as well as the necessity of existence, attributed to a subject.[19]

This is to say that "possibility" in the second[20] sense is applicable to a thing, both in the denial of that thing and in its affirmation. So that it is possible for the thing to be, and possible for it not to be, that is, not impossible to be and not impossible not to be. /

273    Since "possibility" in the second sense[21] is applicable to both aspects of a thing,[22] it is properly designated by the name "possibility." The necessary in existence does not enter this type of possibility, according to which things are either [1] possible, [2] necessary in existence, or [3] impossible. But according to the first

---

[18] In *Naj.* (pp. 17-18), "possibility" in this sense is referred to as "common," "general" or "popular" (*al-'āmma*). This is also the name given to it in the present work (see, for example, p. 285). This type of possibility is a genus for necessity of existence and not a synonymous name for it. For necessity of existence is other than impossibility – and what is not impossible is possible in this sense. But "possibility" in this sense is applicable to whatever is not impossible, be that necessary in existence or not. Hence possibility in this sense is more general than necessity of existence.

[19] This sense of "possibility" has been agreed upon by the elite or the specialists (*al-khāṣṣa*) (ibid.). This is what Ibn Sīnā calls "possibility in the real sense" or "real possibility." When "possibility" is used by Ibn Sīnā with no qualification, it is this type of possibility that is intended.

[20] Text: *al-imkān al-awwal* ("possibility" in the first sense).

[21] Text: *al-imkān bil-ma'nā al-awwal* ("possibility" in the first sense).

[22] I.e., to the negation of the necessity of non-existence as well as to the negation of the necessity of existence.

comprehension [of "possibility," things are] either [1] possible or [2] impossible.

Thus, according to the second and proper comprehension, "the non-possible" has the same meaning as that of "not non-necessary."[23] Hence the necessary in existence is not possible in this sense. /

The possible in this sense includes the existent whose necessity of existence does not endure, even though it has necessity at some time, such as the eclipse.[24]

[3] The term "possible" may be understood in a third sense which seems more proper than the first two types already mentioned. According to this sense the judgment is not necessary in a real sense,[25] nor in time, as the eclipse; nor in [some] state, as the change for the movable.[26] But it is like writing for the human being.[27] /

---

[23] *Ghayr mā lais bi-ḍarūriyy*. The possible, in the second sense, is what is non-necessary. The non-possible would, then, be the not non-necessary, i.e., the necessary.

[24] Ibn Sīnā makes the point here that when he says "'possibility' in the second sense" we are to understand the negation of real necessity only. Unreal necessity is not negated by this type of possibility, but is subsumed under it. As concrete things are called "necessary," in an unreal sense, they are also called "possible" but their possibility is not pure: some degree of necessity has already been attached to them.

[25] *Al-batta* (at all). If we are to read this "... the judgment is not necessary at all," then there would be no need to make the addition that Ibn Sīnā makes, namely, that this is so, nor in time nor in a certain state, both of which are types of conditioned necessity. In other words, "... necessity at all" covers all types of necessity; but the addition of the last two phrases indicates that not all types of necessity have been covered by the necessity mentioned in the first part of the sentence.

[26] "Nor in time" refers to the last three types of conditioned necessity, 2C, 2D and 2E, mentioned in the second chapter of the present method. And "nor in a certain state" refers to the conditioned necessity of type 2B.

[27] "Writing" for "human being" endures without necessity. Even though "writing" is necessary, in an unreal sense, for "human being" as long as he writes, it is not necessary in any sense that a human being writes. For "writing" attaches to "human being" accidentally. Conceptually there is no necessary link between "human being" and "writing." But when one sits down and writes, i.e., in existence, there is a necessary link between the subject and the predicate, as long as the predicate endures in existence for the subject.

This third type of possibility is said by Ibn Sīnā to have the most proper sense of "possibility" – the reason being its complete freedom from any type of necessity. Even though possibility in this third sense is given, in the present work, as a separate type of possibility, it is not mentioned at all in the discussion on possibility in *Naj.* (pp. 17-19). In *Man.* (p. 73), this type of possibility is mentioned, but there it is considered as a species of the second or proper sense of possibility.

275    There are, then, four considerations: [1] a necessary in existence, [2] an impossible, [3] an existent having some necessity, and [4] a thing without any necessity. Or

[4] finally, the term "possible" may be understood in another sense. In considering "the possible" in this sense, attention is not paid to that by which a thing is qualified in one of the states of [its] existence, whether affirmatively or negatively. Rather, attention is paid in respect of its future state. Thus if [by] this sense we are to understand the non-necessary in existence, or in non-existence, at any time it is supposed in the future, it is, then, possible.[28] /

276    He who makes it a condition [of the possible] in this sense that it be non-existent at the present, makes an undesirable condition. This is so because he believes that if he makes it exist, he gives it necessity of existence. However, he does not know that if he does not make it exist, but supposes it as non-existent, he, then, gives it necessity of non-existence. If this is not harmful, that is not harmful either.[29]

277    *Chapter Four. Remark: Concerning principles and conditions for the modes*

Here are some things you must pay attention to:

You must know that existence does not prevent possibility. How [could it prevent it], when [1] necessary existence is subsumed under the first type of possibility; [2] possibility in the second sense is applicable to that which exists with a conditioned necessity; and [3] that which exists at the present does not negate that which does not exist at a later time, let alone that whose existence and non-existence

---

[28] To summarize the findings of this chapter so far, the first type of possibility, "possibility" in the general sense, is a negation of impossibility. Possibility of the second type, "possibility" in the proper sense, is a negation of both impossibility and necessity of existence – taking "necessity" in the real sense. The third type of possibility, "possibility" in the most proper sense, is a negation of impossibility, real necessity of existence, as well as unreal necessity. The fourth type of possibility, future possibility, is a negation of future necessity.

[29] I.e., if necessity of non-existence does not prevent future possibility, then necessity of existence does not prevent it either. Indeed, neither of them does.

are not necessary? For it is not the case that if a thing moves at the present, it is impossible for it not to move at a future time, let alone if it is not necessary for it to move or not to move at every moment in the future. /

You must know that what endures is other than the necessary. Thus, writing may always be negated of a certain individual at the time of his existence, let alone at the time of his non-existence, without that negation being necessary.

Further, you must know that the necessary negative proposition is other than that which negates necessity; the possible negative proposition is other than that which negates possibility; and the concrete negative proposition which is without duration is other than that which negates existence without duration.[30]

These things and the detailed comprehension of the possible are rarely discerned, something which causes much error.

---

[30] Ibn Sīnā draws attention here to the distinction between a negative modal proposition and a proposition whose mode is negated. Take, for example, a necessary negative proposition and a proposition whose necessity is negated. In the former, it is the statement itself that is negated, but the necessity is affirmed: "It is necessary that A is not B." It is the subject-predicate relation that is negated, but it is affirmed that the negation of this relation cannot be otherwise. In the latter, on the other hand, it is the necessity itself that is negated, but the statement is affirmed. In other words, the subject-predicate relation is affirmed, but it is affirmed as not incapable of being otherwise: "It is not necessary that A is B." Here, it is affirmed that A is B, but what is negated is that this is so always.

Similarly, a possible negative proposition is one in which the subject-predicate relation is negated but the possibility of this negation is affirmed while a negative possible proposition is one in which the subject-predicate relation is affirmed, but the possibility of this affirmation is negated. Here is an example of the former: "It is possible that A is not B." And an example of the latter is: "It is not possible that A is B."

Finally, to say "It is concretely that A is not B," is to negate the relation of A to B, but to affirm that this negation is concretely so. If instead you say, "It is not concretely that A is B," you affirm the relation of A to B, but you negate that this affirmation is concretely so.

In Arabic, the test of whether a modal proposition is negative or whether it is one whose mode is negated is simple: this is determined by the place of the negative particle with respect to the mode. If the negative particle precedes the mode, it is the mode that is negated; but if the negative particle is preceded by the mode, it is the statement itself that is negated.

280    *Chapter Five. Remark: Concerning the determination of the universal affirmative in the modes*

You must know that if we say, "Every C is B," we do not mean by this that the universality of C is B, or the universal C is B. Rather, what we mean by this is that every one of that which is qualified as C – be it so qualified in a mental assumption or in external existence, and be it so qualified always or not always, i.e., in just any
282 manner – / is a thing qualified by B without adding that it is qualified by B at such and such a time, in such and such a state or always. For all of this is more specific for C than being qualified by B absolutely. This is, then, the meaning of the statement, "Every C is B," without addition of one of the modes. It is in this sense [that the statement] is called "absolute, common and definite." But if we add anything else
283 to it, we give it modality. / An example of a statement with such an addition is, "Necessarily every C is B," as if saying, "Every one of that which is qualified as C, always or not always, is, as long as its essence exists, B by necessity. But if, for example, it is not C, then we do not posit as a condition that it be B by necessity, as long as it is qualified as C; but something more general than that."[31] Another example is the statement, "Every C is always B;" as if saying "Every one of the things which is C according to the previously mentioned manner[32] is found to have B always, as long as its essence exists, yet without necessity."

As for the question, "Is this universal affirmative predication true in every case, or is it always false? In other words, is it possible for that which is not necessary to be always present in every individual,
284 or is it always negated of every individual? / Or is this not possible, and that which is not necessary must unavoidably be present in some individuals and must unavoidably be negated of some others?" is a matter concerning which the logician need not make any judgment.

It is not a condition of the proposition with which the logician is concerned that it be true. Sometimes he is also concerned with that which is nothing but false.

Again, an example of a statement [having an addition] is, "Every one of the things called C, in accordance with the preceding manner,

---

[31] I.e., more general than necessity: and that is, duration without necessity.
[32] According to duration without necessity.

is called B, not as long as its essence exists but at a determined time, such as the eclipse, or at a non-determined time, such as respiration for the human being." Or it is called C in a state that does not endure, as when we say, "Every movable changes." These are the various types of concrete propositions. /

285    Another example is the statement, "Every one of the things called C, in accordance with the preceding manner, may be qualified by B according to 'possibility' taken in the general, the proper or the most proper sense."

According to the method of some, the statement, "Every C is B in existence or in something else," [33] has another aspect.[34] This is its meaning: "Every C, at the present or in the past, has been qualified by B at the time of its existence." The statement, "Every C is B," is, then,
286    necessary and / is applicable to the three times.[35]

And if we say, for example, "Every C is B, according to 'possibility' taken in the most specific sense," [36] this, then, means, "Every C, at any supposed time in the future, can be correctly qualified as B and as not B." We do not mind paying attention to this consideration, even though the former is the appropriate one.[37]

---

[33] *Wa-ghayrih* (and something other than it), by which is meant "or in non-existence."

[34] An aspect other than possibility.

[35] If C has existed or exists as B, it is necessary that C is B, and this cannot be otherwise even in the future. This is the view indicated on p. 276 of the present method. But as we have seen, Ibn Sīnā opposes this view by saying if actual existence, be that past or present, renders the object necessary and hence prevents future possibility, then actual non-existence does the same; but the truth is that neither of them has any bearing on future possibility.

[36] *Al-akhaṣṣ* (more proper, most proper, more specific, most specific). It has been translated here as "most specific" rather than "most proper" for the following reason. We learn from *Man.*, p. 73 that what is referred to as "possibility" in the most proper sense is what has been called, in the present method, the third type of possibility, and not future possibility, of which the term is used here. Future possibility, on the other hand, is to be taken into consideration but not to be thought of as the most appropriate type of possibility. The last statement of the present chapter confirms this.

[37] In other words, Ibn Sīnā takes into consideration future possibility, yet he knows that the most appropriate type of possibility is what has been classified in the present method as the third type of possibility.

### Chapter Six. Remark: Concerning the determination of the universal negative in the modes

In accordance with what has been considered, you know that in the universal negative absolute with common application, which is required by this type of absolute, it is necessary that the negation be applicable to every one of the things described as subject in the previously mentioned manner, such that no time or state is specified.[38] It is as if saying, "Of every one of the things which is C, B is denied," without specifying the time or state of the denial.

But the languages that we know usually lacked the use of the universal negation in this form. They have used for the universal negative definiteness an expression indicating a meaning additional to what is required by this type of absolute. Thus in Arabic they say "*Lā shay' min jīm bā'*" (Nothing of C is B). For the Arabs this requires that nothing of that which is C can be at all described as B as long as it is described as C. This is a negation applicable to every one of the things described as C as long as it is subject for [C], and until[39] it ceases to be subject for it.[40] Similarly, it is said in classical Persian, "*Hīch jīm bā nīst*" (None of the things which is C is B). This use embraces the necessary[41] and one of the types of the absolute whose condition is in the subject.[42] This has also led many people to error on the side of the affirmative universal.

But the words that best express the universal negative absolute, with common application, are equivalent to the statement, "Every C

---

[38] The text here reads "such that no state or time is specified." We made this switch for the sake of consistency in this chapter. It should also be mentioned that one of the manuscripts as listed by Dunyā makes the same switch (see *Ish.*; Part I, p. 287).

[39] *Illā* (except). We suppose it "*ilā.*"

[40] And thus a universal negative proposition ceases to be absolute, in the sense of "non-modal." For it is now necessary: it requires (1) the duration of the subject's being qualified by C (unreal necessity: more precisely, the necessity of type B); and (2) that the subject has the same essence (type A of conditioned necessity: a kind of real necessity). The subject must be qualified by C, but that is not sufficient for this negation to hold; the subject's essence must also endure. This is made clear after we are given another example from classical Persian.

[41] I.e., the necessary which is conditioned by the duration of the essence of the subject.

[42] I.e., unreal necessity of type B.

is not B," or "B is negated of [every C] , without specifying a time or state."

The concrete negative proposition, i.e., the specific absolute, is what is equivalent to the statement, "Every C is something of which B is denied, in a non-necessary and non-enduring manner."

In necessity there is no gap between the two sides.[43] The difference between the two is that the statement, "Every C is by necessity not B," makes "necessity" belong to the state of the negation of every one [of C], / while the statement, "By necessity nothing of C is B," makes "necessity" belong to the general negation and to its definiteness, and does not apply to every one [of C] except in potentiality. Thus in spite of the difference in meaning, there is no difference in the consequence of the two statements. But where one is appropriate, the other is [also] appropriate.[44]

Along this line, judge [the universal negative] involving possibility.

## Chapter Seven. Admonition: Concerning points of disagreement and agreement between the consideration of the mode and that of predication

You must known that "absoluteness" of the mode and "absoluteness" of predication are different in meaning and in consequence. For one

---

[43] *Al-jihatain* (aspects, sides, modes). These are the two manners of representing the universal negative proposition: "Every C is not B," and "Nothing of C is B." To translate "*al-jihatain*" here by "modes," as Goichon does (*Dir. Rem.*, p. 147), will not do; whether the reference is to the two forms of universal negation by themselves, or whether the reference is to the necessity involved in these two forms. If the former, then this rendering is incorrect because the two forms of the universal negation by themselves are free from modality. And if the latter, this rendering is still incorrect because the mode involved in both statements is necessity, which is to say, there is one rather than two modes.

[44] What is intended here is that even though "Every C is not B" is better fit to give absolute universal negation – "absolute" in the sense of "non-modal" – then "Nothing of C is B;" when these two statements involve necessity, they can be used interchangeably, even though they differ in meaning. The difference in meaning between them is this: when "Every C is not B" involves necessity, it says that it is necessary that the negation is actually applicable to every individual C; but when "Nothing of C is B" involves necessity, it says that it is necessary that the negation is applicable to all Cs in general, without touching upon every C individually, except potentially. It is because of this potential equivalence that the two statements can be used interchangeably, in spite of the difference in meaning between their actual states.

of them may be true without the other being so. For example, if there is a time at which it happens that there is no black human being, then "Every human being is white" is true at that time by judgment of the mode, but not by judgment of predication.

The same is also true of possibility of the mode. Thus if[45] at a certain time it is assumed, for example, that there is no color except white or another one of the infinite number of colors, the statement "Every color is white or such other color," is then true in an absolute sense by virtue of the absoluteness of the mode; before that, it was possible. But this possibility is not true if linked to the predicate. For it is not by proper possibility that every color is white. Rather, there are colors that are by necessity not white.

Similarly, if we assume that at a certain time there is no animal except the human being, then "Every animal is a human being" is true at that time in accordance with the absolute sense of the mode. Before that, [this was] in possibility. But this cannot be in possibility if possibility is made to belong to the predicate.[46]

Along this line, judge the possible.

292    *Chapter Eight. Remark: Concerning the determination of the two particular propositions and the modes*

You know that the state of the two particular propositions is from the two universal ones, and you judge the former by [the rules of] the latter. The statement, "Some C is B," is true even if that "some" is described as B at some time and not at another. Further, you know that if each "some" is described thus, then this ["description"] is true of every "some." And if the affirmation is true of every "some," then it is true of every individual. From this you know that it is not a condition of absolute affirmation that it be applicable to every number at every moment. The same is true of negation. /

293    You must know that if "Some C is by necessity B" is true, this does not require the prevention of the following statement from being true: "Some C is B, in a non-necessary absolute sense, or in possibility." But the converse is not true. You say, "Some bodies are by necessity

---

[45] *Fa-innahu* (thus, it is). We suppose it *"fa-in,"* as does Forget, p. 40.
[46] *Idhā ju'il al-maḥmūl* (if it is made the predicate). We are reading *"li-lmaḥmūl"* instead of *"al-maḥmūl."*

movable," that is, as long as the essence of that "some" exists; "Some are movable by a non-necessary existence;" and "Some are [such] by a non-necessary possibility."

294 *Chapter Nine. Remark: Concerning the implication of modal propositions*

You must know that the statement, "By necessity it is," is of the same force as the statement, "It is not possible – taking 'possibility' in the popular sense – that it is not," which in turn is of the same force as 295 the statement, "It is impossible that it is not." / And the statement, "By necessity it is not," is of the same force as the statement,"It is not possible – taking 'possibility' in the general sense – that it is," which is of the same force as the statement, "It is impossible that it is." [In] each order,[47] these propositions are implied by those which are parallel to them and are interchangeable with them.

As for the possible statement whose "possibility" is in the proper sense, and that whose "possibility" is in the most proper sense, there are no statements that they imply, and that are equivalent to them, of the two types of necessity.[48] Rather, they imply statements of the modal type which are more general than they and which are not convertible with them. It is not necessary that every implied statement be equivalent [to that which implies it]. Thus the statement, "By necessity it is," implies the following statement: "It is possible that it is," taking "possibility" in the general sense; yet it is not convertible with it. For it is not the case that if it is possible that it is, it must, therefore, by necessity be; but perhaps it is possible also that it is not. The statement, "By necessity it is not," implies the following statement: "It is possible that it is not," taking "possibility" in the general sense also; and again without convertibility [between the two] – the explication is the same.[49]

Further, you must know that the statement, "It is possible that it is," taking "possibility" in the proper sense and in the most proper

---

[47] These are the orders of necessity, possibility and impossibility.

[48] I.e., necessity of non-existence, and necessity of existence.

[49] I.e., as the previous one, where it was explained that a statement which is implied by another may not be convertible with it, if the former includes but is more general than the latter.

296 sense, / implies only the following statement: "It is possible that it is not," according to the same type of possibility. [These two statements] are equivalent. As for [the possible statement] whose possibility is of another type, it does not imply that which is equivalent to it, but that which is more general than it, such as "It is possible that it is," taking "possibility" in the general sense; and "It is possible that it is not," taking "possibility" in the same sense. What is implied by this is, "It is not necessary in existence that it is;" "It is not necessary in existence that it is not." And "It is not impossible that it is;" "It is not impossible that it is not." In short, "It is not necessary that it is;" "It is not necessary that it is not."

297 *Chapter Ten. Delusion and Admonition*

The problem that a group of people raise to create fear is the following: "If the necessary in existence is possible of being, and [if] the possible of being is possible of non-being, then the necessary in existence is possible of non-being." And, "If the necessary in existence is not possible of being, and [if] that which is not possible is impossible of being, then the necessary is impossible of being."

It is not exceptionally difficult to solve this problem. For the necessary in existence is possible of being, according to "possibility" in the general sense. But it does not follow from this "possible" that it be convertible with "possible of non-being." The necessary in existence is not possible in the proper sense. And from the statement, "It is not possible in this sense,"[50] it does not follow that it is impossible. Because that which is not possible in this sense is that 298 which is necessary, either affirmatively or negatively. / Even though such people are well aware of the doubt [concerning the seriousness of this problem], and expect to be given a solution for it, they, nevertheless, repeat their error. Thus whenever they find it true of a thing that it is not possible, or they suppose it thus, they think that it follows from this that by necessity it is not. Building on this [misunderstanding], they continue in error. For they do not remember that it need not be the case that that which is not possible, in the proper and most proper sense, by necessity is not; but

---

[50] I.e., the proper one.

sometimes by necessity it is.[51] Similarly, sometimes they err greatly by believing that if one supposes that a thing is not by necessity, it follows that it is a real possible,[52] convertible with that which is possible of non-being. But that is not so. You had already learned this among the things to which we have guided you on the right path.

[51] Text: *biḍ-ḍarūra lais* (by necessity it is not).
[52] I.e., possible in the proper sense.

# The Fifth Method

## On the Contradiction and Conversion of Propositions

*A general word concerning contradiction*

You must know that contradiction is the differing of two propositions in affirmation and negation, in a manner requiring essentially that one of the two propositions be true – whether in itself or not in itself – and the other be false. So that truth and falsity are inherently present in the two propositions, even though this is indeterminate, according to the unlearned, in some possible propositions. /

There is opposition in affirmation and negation only when the negative of the two propositions / negates the affirmed one, [just in the sense in which] it is affirmed. For if a thing is affirmed and it is not true, then the meaning of "It is not true" is that the thing is not as it is affirmed. Conversely, if a thing is negated and it is not true, then the meaning of "It is not true" is that the contradictory of the affirmation is false.

But it may have been that one is distracted from considering the contradiction, due to being distracted from considering the opposition. In considering the opposition, you consider, in each of the two propositions, what you consider in the other. So that the parts of each of the two propositions are the same as those in the other and have the same conditions as those of the other.[1] Thus [the following items in one proposition] are not different in meaning [from those in the other]:

[1] subject and predicate, and what resembles them;[2]
[2] condition and relation; /
[3] part and whole;
[4] potentiality and actuality;

---

[1] Text: *wa-'alā mā fī al-ukhrā* (having the same state as the other, or are in the same state as the other).

[2] That is, the antecedent and consequent.

[5] place and time; and other [conditions] that have been enumerated. /

If the proposition is not singular, then the two propositions must also differ in quantity – I mean, in universality and particularity – as they differ in quality – I mean, in affirmation and negation – otherwise it would be possible for the two propositions not to partition truth and falsity. Instead they would be false together, such as the two universal propositions when their matter is possible.³ Here is an example: "Every human being is a writer," and "Not one human being is a writer." Or the two propositions would be true together, such as the two particular propositions when their matter is also possible.⁴ An example of this is: "Some human beings are writers," and "Some human beings are not writers." But in definite propositions, after the previously-mentioned conditions have been satisfied, the contradiction is not completed except if one of the two propositions is universal and the other particular. / After these conditions have been satisfied, there may be need in modal propositions of [other] conditions for the realization of the contradiction.⁵

Let the affirmative proposition first be universal. And let us consider [it] in the matters.⁶ Thus if we say,

"Every human being is an animal," "Some human beings are not animals;" ⁷

"Every human being is a writer," "Some human beings are not writers;" ⁸

"Every human being is a stone," and "Some human beings are not stones;" ⁹

we find that one of the two propositions [in each pair] is true and the other false – even though the true in the necessary [matter] is other than that in the other two [matters].

Now let the negative proposition be also universal. And similarly, let us consider [it] in the matters. Thus, if we say,

---

³ Text: *fī māddat al-imkān* (in the matter of possibility).
⁴ Text: *fī māddat al-imkān aiḍan* (in the matter of possibility also).
⁵ Text: *taḥaqquqihā*. The pronoun at the end of *taḥaqquq* refers to "mode," so that the sentence would read: "... the realization of the mode."
⁶ I.e., necessity, possibility and impossibility.
⁷ These two statements are in the matter of necessity.
⁸ These two statements are in the matter of possibility.
⁹ These two statements are in the matter of impossibility.

"Not one human being is an animal," "Some human beings are animals;" [10]

"Not one human being being is a stone," "Some human beings are stones;" [11]

"Not one human being is a writer," and "Some human beings are writers;" [12]

we find that the partitioning [of the truth and falsity] also obtains.

Now you yourself consider the true and the false in every matter, and the parallels between propositions differing in quality and quantity.

307 *Chapter One. Remark: Concerning the contradiction between absolute propositions, and the determination of the contradictory of absolute and concrete propositions*

Due to distortion and little reflection, people may judge that the absolute proposition has a contradictory among the absolute propositions. They do not consider, except the difference in quality and quantity. They do not reflect enough on how it is possible that there are states of other conditions, in order for the opposition to obtain.

Thus if what is intended by the statement "Every C is B," that is, "Every one of C is B," without adding "at every time," then what is intended is to affirm B of every unit [of C], without adding that this judgment is true of every one [of C] at every time. If this is not prevented, then it is not necessary that the statement, "Every C is B," is contradicted by the statement, "Some C is not B," so that if one statement is false, the other is true, and vice-versa.[13] /

308 Indeed, it is not necessary that its contrary[14] – I mean the universal negation – does not agree with it in truth. For if the affirmation which is applicable to every individual is not accompanied by the

---

[10] These two statements are in the matter of necessity.
[11] These two statements are in the matter of impossibility.
[12] These two statements are in the matter of possibility.
[13] In other words, if the statement, "Every C is B," is allowed to be freed from the condition "at every time," then it is not contradicted by the statement, "Some C is not B." This is to say that the mere difference in quality and quantity between two absolute propositions is not sufficient to make them contradictory of each other.
[14] I.e., the contrary of the statement, "Every C is B."

condition "at every time," then it is possible for the negation which is applicable to every, or to some individuals, to be true with the affirmation – if [the negation] is not at every time.

Rather, it is necessary that the contradictory of the statement, "Every C is B," taken in the most general absolute sense, is "Some C is always not B." And the contradictory of the statement, "Nothing of C is B," which is in the sense of "B is denied of every C," without addition,[15] is the statement, "Some C is always B." You know the difference between this enduring proposition and the necessary one. The contradictory of the statement, "Some C is B," taken in this absolute sense, is the statement, "B is always negated of C." And this corresponds to the expression used in universal negation which is "Nothing of C is B," taken in accordance with the already-mentioned customary use.[16] And the contradictory of the statement, "Some C is not B," is the statement, "Every C is always B." /

309 As for the absolute proposition which is the more specific – this is the proposition which we have exclusively designated by the name
310 "concrete proposition" – / if we use it to say, "Every C is B," in the manner we have indicated, then its contradictory is, "Concretely only, every C is not B." That is, either "By necessity some C is B," or "B is denied of [some C]." And if we employ the concrete proposition to say, "Nothing of C is B," in the manner previously indicated, then the contradictory opposite of this is what is understood by the statement, "Of some C, B is always affirmed or denied." For if the judgment has preceded as "Of every C, B is denied, sometime and not always," then the statement which is the opposite [contradictory] of this is only one which denies it always or affirms it always. We do
311 not find / a proposition which does not have a counterpart or whose counterpart is difficult to find. The contradictory of the statement, "Some C is B," in the manner under consideration, is "Nothing of C is B, concretely only." And the contradictory of the statement, "Some C is not B," which is the negation [of "Some C is B"], in the same sense, is the statement, "Every C is either always B, or always not B."

Do not think that the statement, "Not in an absolute sense, something of C is B" – which is the contrary of the statement, "In an absolute sense, something of C is B" – has the same meaning as the

---

[15] Addition of the condition "at every time."
[16] That is, always.

statement, "In an absolute sense, nothing of C is B." For the former statement may be true with the statement, "By necessity, every C is B," but the latter cannot. /

312     If we want to find for the absolute proposition a contradictory of the same genus, then the procedure is to make the absolute proposition more specific than that which is required by the same affirmation or negation, taken in an absolute sense. This is exemplified by making the universal affirmative absolute proposition one in which the judgment is not only applicable to every individual, but also at every time in which the subject is qualified by that which has qualified it or was made to accompany it, as one must comprehend by the usual sense of expressing the judgment in the universal negative. So that the statement, "Every C is B," is true only if every one of C is B at every time in which C is and at every moment. Such that if at a certain moment a thing is qualified as C by necessity or by non-necessity, yet at that moment it is not qualified as B, the statement is then false, as one comprehends by the expression customarily used for the
313 universal negation. If we agree / on this, then the statement, "Some C is not B, in an absolute sense," is the contradictory of the statement, "Every C is B." And the statement, "Some C is B, in an absolute sense," is the contradictory of the universal negative.

But we would have posited a condition additional to what is required by the pure affirmation and pure negation. Yet in spite of that, no absolute in the concrete sense is necessitated by this
314 condition. / For it is not the case that, if every C is B at every moment it is C, therefore, by necessity it is B as long as its essence exists. You have already learned this.

Those who have preceded us cannot, by their examples and their use, agree with us on that. But the explication of this is much too long. /

315     If the procedure is also to make the statement, "Every C is B," such that only a specific time is intended in it, a time which is not common to every one or to every individual C but [only] to every C existing at that time – the same being true of the statement, "Nothing of C is B," [in which what is intended] are the Cs that exist at a specific time[17] – then if we preserve that specific time in the two particular

---

[17] Text: *min jīmāt zamān mawjūd bi-'aynih* (are Cs of a specific time that exists).

propositions after [preserving] the rest of what must be preserved, and whose preservation is easy, the contradiction obtains. /

316 A group of people have judged this to be so. But they were unable to continue paying attention to this principle. Again, they found themselves in need of shying away from the consideration of beneficial conditions. For a determination of this, one should refer to *Kitāb ash-Shifā'*.

317 *Chapter Two. Remark: Concerning contradiction in the remaining modal propositions*

As for the enduring proposition, the contradiction for it is produced in the same manner as that of the concrete proposition, [taken] in accordance with the first procedure. And it is close to it. Learn [the procedure] from that.

The statement, "By necessity, every C is B," has as a contradictory: "Not by necessity, every C is B." This is to say, "Rather it is possible, taking 'possibility' in the most general and not in the most specific or
318 proper sense, that some C is not B." / What is implied by it is what is implied by this possibility in this place.[18] The statement, "By necessity, nothing of C is B," has as a contradictory: "Not by necessity, nothing of C is B." That is, "It is possible that some C is B, taking 'possibility' in that sense[19] and not in another." The statement, "By necessity, some C is B," is opposed, along the lines indicated, by the statement, "It is possible that nothing of C is B, taking 'possibility' in the most general sense." What negates this possibility does not imply what affirms it, and what affirms it does not imply what negates it.[20] Keep this in mind, and do not forget it as did the Ancients.

The statement, "It is possible that every C is B, taking 'possibility' in the most general sense," is opposed, in the manner of a contradictory,
319 by the statement, "It is not possible that every C is B," / which implies "By necessity, some C is not B." Now you yourself complete the

---

[18] That is, what is implied by "Not by necessity, every C is B" is the same as what is implied by "It is possible that some C is not B, taking 'possibility' in the most general, or in the popular sense."

[19] I.e., in the most general sense.

[20] As is the case with "possibility" taken in the proper sense. There it is true to say, "It is," and "It is not."

remaining divisions[21] along the lines already indicated, and which you have learned.

The statement, "It is possible that every C is B, taking 'possibility' in the proper sense," is opposed by the statement, "It is not possible that every C is B." This does not imply "that is impossible" more than it implies "that is necessary in existence." Rather, it does not imply any kind of necessity. This you must retain. The statement, "It is possible that nothing of C is B according to this kind of possibility," is opposed by the statement, "It is not possible that nothing of C is B." As if he who says this says, "Rather, it is necessary in existence that something of C is B," or "It is impossible...." Again, as if he says, "By necessity, some C is B," or "By necessity, some C is not B." There is no common element that these two statements[22] share to immediately enable us to make an affirmative statement about it so that the contradictory of the possible negative would be affirmative. Further, what need is there for that [when] it is known that the statement, "It is possible that it is not" is, in truth, an affirmation? / In addition to this, the statement, "It is possible that some C is B according to this sense of possibility," has as a contradictory the statement, "It is not possible that some C is B." That is, either "It is necessary that it is" or "It is necessary that it is not." And the statement, "It is possible that some C is not B," has as a contradictory, the statement, "It is not possible that some C is not B." That is, "By necessity, every C is B," or "By necessity, nothing of C is B."

This is how you must comprehend the state of contradiction of modal propositions. And cast aside what others say.

*Chapter Three. Remark: Concerning the conversion of absolute propositions*

Conversion is the rendering of the predicate of a proposition as the subject, and the subject as the predicate, while retaining the quality, truth and falsity as they are. /

It is customary to begin with the conversion of the universal absolute negative, and to show that it is converted to itself. The truth

---

[21] I.e., the remaining possible propositions, whose "possibility" is taken in the most general sense.

[22] Text: *al-amrain* (two matters, or two things).

is that it does not have a conversion, except by some procedures already-mentioned. Thus it is possible to negate, in an actual manner, "laughter" of every individual human being; but this does not necessitate the negation of "human being" of anything that laughs. For a thing which does not exist except in a certain thing may be negated, in an absolute manner, of that certain thing without its being possible to negate the latter of the former. /

323   The reasoning of some does not necessitate, except that the absolute proposition be taken under one of the other two aspects.[23] This is how this reasoning procedes.

If we say, "Nothing of C is B," this necessitates that the following absolute proposition, "Nothing of B is C," is true; otherwise the contradictory which is the following absolute proposition, "Some C is B," will be true. Let us suppose that this "some" is a specific thing,
324   and let it be D. Then D itself is C and B at the same time. / Thus something which is C is B – this something being B, the supposed object. Not that the affirmative particular conversion makes it affirmative, for we have not yet learned the conversion of the affirmative particular. But we have said, "Nothing of C is B." This is impossible.

The response to this reasoning is that this is not impossible, if the
325   negation is taken / in an absolute, and not in a usual sense only. You have already learned that, in absoluteness,[24] both[25] are true as it is true to negate, in an absolute manner, actual laughter of every individual human being and to affirm it of some. /

326   Taken under the other two absolute aspects,[26] the universal negative converts to itself, according to this same reasoning. /

329   As for their recent reasoning, which is in accordance with the method of divergence, introduced after the first teacher,[27] there is no need for us to mention it. For, even though certain people may think well of it, it is falsified. We had already shown its case in *Kitāb ash-Shifā'*. /

---

[23] I.e., aspects of absoluteness: the common and the specific, the non-modal and that which has been called "concrete."

[24] Text: *al-muṭlaq* (absolute proposition).

[25] I.e., the following two propositions: "Absolutely, nothing of C is B," and "Absolutely, some C is B."

[26] The other two absolute aspects are the common and the specific.

[27] I.e., Aristotle.

330  The universal affirmative must not convert to a universal proposition. For the predicate may be more general than the subject. Nor also must it convert to a pure absolute proposition, without necessity. Since the predicate may not be necessary for the subject, while the subject is necessary for the predicate, such as respiration for the animal that has lungs. Respiration is concrete and of non-enduring concomitance [for such an animal]. But the latter is necessary for respiration. For every being that respires is by necessity an animal that has lungs.

An absolute proposition converts only to a general absolute, capable of receiving[28] necessity.

But the affirmative universal can, without doubt, be converted to an affirmative particular. Thus if "Every C is B," then we must be able to find a specific thing which is C and B. This C will then be B. And this B will be C.

331  Similarly, the affirmative particular converts to itself. / And if the affirmative universal and the affirmative particular are among the absolute propositions which have a contradictory of the same genus, then it can be shown that they convert to a particular in the following
333  way: if it is not true that some B is C, then nothing of B is C, / from which it follows that nothing of C is B.

As for the negative particular, it does not convert. For it is possible that "Every C is not B" when "Every B is C," it is not the case that "Every B is not C." For example, it is true that some human beings do not actually laugh, and it is not possible that none of the things which actually laugh is a human being.

334  *Chapter Four. Remark: Concerning the conversion of necessary propositions*

As for the necessary universal negative, it converts to itself. For if B were by necessity negated of every C, and [if] it were then possible to find some B which is C and to suppose it, this would convert to "Some C is B" in accordance with the requirement of the absolute sense which is common to the necessary and others. But this is not at all true with the universal necessary negation. Rather, it is impossible that they are true together. Thus that to which this has led is an

---

[28] *Taḥtamil.*

335 impossibility. It is for you to show this by hypothesis. / Thus make this "some" D; then you find that some of what is C has become B, when it had been posited that "Nothing of C is B." This is impossible.

The necessary affirmative universal converts to an affirmative particular, in accordance with what has been shown of the judgment of the absolute proposition, with common application. But it must not convert to a necessary proposition. For it is possible that the
336 conversion of a necessary proposition is to a possible one. / But it is possible that C, such as "laughter," has B, such as "human being," as necessary for it; while B, such as "human being," has C, such as "laughter," as non-necessary for it. Do not believe him who says anything else and attempts to play tricks concerning this matter. Thus the necessary affirmative universal converts [to a possible proposition] whose "possibility" is taken in the most general sense.

The necessary affirmative particular also converts to a particular
337 along the same lines. / And the necessary negative particular does not convert, for the reason you already know. An example of this is "By necessity, every animal is not a human being." But "Every human being is an animal." Then it is not the case that "Every human being is not an animal."

338 *Chapter Five. Remark: Concerning the conversion of possible propositions*

As for the possible propositions, they must not have a conversion in negation. For it is not the case that, if "It is not impossible, but possible, that no human being writes," it must be that "It is possible, and not impossible, that none of those who write is a human being; or that some of those who write are not human beings."

Similarly, this example shows the case of the possible, in the proper and the most proper senses. For it is possible to deny one thing of another, but not conversely, because the latter is the proper subject of the former, and the former does not occur except to the latter. /
339 The possible propositions in affirmation must have conversion. But the proper possible must not convert to itself. Do not listen to him who says that "If a thing is possible, and not necessary for its subject, then its subject is the same with respect to it." Reflect on how that which moves voluntarily is among what is possible for the animal, and how the animal is necessary for it.

Do not pay attention to the efforts made by a certain group concerning this matter. Rather, all types of the possible in affirmation convert, according to the most general possibility. Thus if "Every C is B in possibility" or "Some C is B in possibility," then "Some B is C in the most general possibility"; otherwise, it is not possible that anything of B is C. / But, as you already know, "By necessity, nothing of B is C" which converts to "By necessity, nothing of C is B." This is absurd.

Someone may say, "Why do you not convert the proper possible negative, since it is of the same force as the affirmative one?" We say that the reason for this is that it – I mean the affirmative one – only converts to an affirmative of the most general type of possibility. And thus the quality would not be preserved.[29] But if its conversion must be to a proper possible, then it would be possible to convert it from an affirmation to a negation. And then the quality would be brought back through the conversion. But this is not [how] the conversion must be.

A certain group claims that the possible particular negative converts, because [the proper possible] particular affirmative, which is of its force, converts – the assumption being that [the latter] also [converts] to a proper [possible], which can be brought back to negation. Their belief is false. You may determine this from what you have already learned. This is illustrated by the statement, "It is possible that some human beings are not laughing creatures;" but you do not say, "It is possible that some of those who laugh are not human beings."

---

[29] I.e., the quality of the proper possible negative.

# The Sixth Method

*Chapter One. Remark: Concerning propositions, with respect to those of them involving assent, and similar ones*[1]

The types of propositions employed by syllogizers and their like[2] are four:[3] [I] admitted propositions, [II] presumed propositions and those

---

[1] In the Ninth Method, we will learn that every type of discourse requires a different type of premise. The present method classifies and discusses the various types of propositions that are employed in the premises of the various types of discourse.

[2] Those resembling syllogizers are those who use induction or analogy.

[3] Here is an outline of these propositions and their subdivisions:
  I. Admitted Propositions (*musullamāt*)
    1. Beliefs (*mu'taqadāt*)
      A. Propositions that must be accepted (*al-wājib qubūluhā*)
        a. Primary propositions (*awwaliyyāt*)
          i. Those which are evident to all (*jaliyyun li-lkull*)
          ii. Those whose evidence may be concealed (*mā rubbamā khafā*)
        b. Observational propositions (*mushāhadāt*)
          i. The sensibles (*al-maḥsusāt*)
          ii. Reflective propositions (*'tibāriyya*)
        c. Experiential propositions (*mujarrabāt*)
        d. Intuited propositions (*al-ḥadsiyyāt*)
        e. Propositions based on unanimous traditions (*muwātarāt*)
        f. Propositions containing syllogisms (*qaḍāiā qiyāsātuhā ma'ahā*)
      B. Widely-known propositions (*al-mashhūrāt*)
        a. Primary propositions and the like (generally acknowledged) (*al-awaliyyāt wa-naḥwahā*)
        b. "Praiseworthy" opinions (*al-maḥmūda*)
      C. Estimative propositions (*al-wahmiyyāt*)
    2. Propositions based on outside sources (*ma'khūdhāt*)
      A. Received propositions (*maqbūlāt*)
      B. Determined propositions (*taqriyyāt*)
  II. Presumed Propositions and Those of the Same Order (*mazūnāt*)
  III. Ambiguous Propositions Resembling Others (*mushabbahāt bi-ghayrihā*)
    1. Resemblance produced by the mediation of an expression
      A. Different in meaning due to the sense of the expression

## CHAPTER 1

of the same order, [III] ambiguous propositions resembling others and [IV] imagined propositions. /

342 [I] Admitted propositions are either [1] beliefs or [2] propositions based on outside sources.

[I.1] Also, beliefs are of three types: [A] propositions that must be accepted, [B] widely-known propositions and [C] estimative propositions. /

343 [I.1.A] Propositions that must be accepted are either [a] primary propositions, [b] observational propositions or [c] experiential propositions, together with [d] intuited propositions, [e] propositions based on transmitted unanimous accounts and [f] containing their

344 syllogisms.[4] / Let us begin by identifying the types of propositions that must be accepted, and the kinds that fall under this group.

[I.1.A.a] The primary propositions are those that are necessitated by the essence and instinct of a clear intellect, and not by any cause external to it.[5] Thus whenever by its essence the intellect conceives

345 the terms of these propositions, it makes an assent. Therefore, / assent in these propositions does not depend except on the occurrence of the concept, and the discernment of [its] composition. Of these

---

        B. Different in meaning due to what occurs to the expression in its composition
        C. Different in meaning due to what occurs to the expression in its declension
    2. Resemblance produced by the mediation of the meaning
        A. Due to imagining the converse
        B. Due to taking the concomitant of a thing instead of that thing
        C. Due to describing a thing by what is accidental to it
  IV. Imagined Propositions (*mukhayyalāt*)
    1. Due to the goodness of the disposition of the statement
    2. Due to the force of its truth
    3. Due to the force of its notoriety
    4. Due to the goodness of its resemblance

[4] *Qaḍāyā qiyāsāt ma'ahā*: literally, propositions with their syllogisms.

[5] These are what Aristotle calls "first principles, basic or primary truths." We are told that both the meaning of the name as well as the existence of these principles is assumed. In other words, they are axiomatic: "I call the basic truths of every genus those elements in it the existence of which cannot be proved. As regards both these primary truths and the attributes dependent on them the meaning of the name is assumed. The fact of their existence as regards the primary truths must be assumed; but it has to be proved of the remainder, the attributes" (Aristotle, *Anal. Post.*, I, 10, 75a, 28-33).

propositions, there are: [i] those which are evident to all, because [their] terms are conceived clearly; and [ii] those [whose evidence] may be concealed, and need reflection on the concealed aspect of the concept of their terms. For if the concept is confused, the assent too is confused. But this division does not present a difficulty for sharp minds that can penetrate the concept.

[I.1.A.b] Observational propositions are of the type[6] of [i] the sensibles – the latter being propositions whose assent is acquired from the [external] sense only. / Examples of these are our judgment that the sun exists and that it shines, and our judgment that fire is hot. Or [ii] they are of the type[7] of reflective propositions[8] produced by the observation of powers other than those of the [external] sense. Examples of such propositions are our knowledge that we have thought, fear and danger, and our awareness of ourselves and the acts of ourselves.

[I.1.A.c] The experientials are propositions and judgments that are consequent upon our repeated observations, which leave a trace by their repetition, thus insuring the formation of a strong and an indubitable belief.[9] It is not incumbent upon the logician to seek the cause of that[10] after the absence of doubt concerning the existence of [this belief is established].

Experience may necessitate a certain judgment, / or it may necessitate a probable one. And it is inevitable that experience has a concealed syllogistic force, mixed with the observations. This is exemplified in our judgment that hitting with wood is painful.

Experience is established only if the soul is assured that the thing is concordant, and to which certain conditions[11] are added. It is then that experience is established. /

---

[6] Text: *ka* (as).

[7] Text: *ka* (as).

[8] *I'tibāriyya*. These propositions are produced by the internal senses, as opposed to those that are produced by the external ones. But both types of propositions are subsumed under "observational propositions."

[9] The formation of experience requires sense-perception. However, not all sense-perception can serve this purpose, but only that which is repeated and whose repetition is preserved in memory (*Naj.*, p. 65; see Aristotle, *Anal. Post.*, II, 19, 99b, 34-40, 100a, 1-6; also, *Meta.*, A, 1).

[10] I.e., the formation of this strong and indubitable belief.

[11] Such as time, place, etc.

## CHAPTER 1      121

348   [I.1.A.d] Among what resembles the experiential propositions are the intuited ones. These are propositions in which the principle of the judgment is a very strong intuition of the soul, with which doubt is removed and to which the mind submits. If one denies that, because one does not take up the consideration required by the power of this intuition, or by way of opposition, one does not achieve what is achieved by him who has this intuition. An example of this is our judgment that the moon gets its light from the sun, in a manner that forms light on it. The intuited propositions too have a syllogistic force; and they are most analogous to the experiential propositions. /

349   [I.1.A.e] Similarly, propositions based on transmitted unanimous accounts are those with which the soul finds full tranquillity, by means of which doubt is removed due to the multiple observations, even though doubt is possible.[12] So that uncertainty regarding the occurrence of these observations in a concordant and a univocal manner is eliminated. This is like our belief in the existence of Makka, Galen, Euclid, and others.

He who tries to limit these observations to a definite numerical figure seeks the impossible. For [propositions based on transmitted unanimous accounts] do not rely on a [specific] number [of observations, not] susceptible to increase and decrease. Rather, they rely only on a figure with which certainty occurs. It is certainty, therefore, that determines the sufficiency of the observations, and not their number. These propositions are also such that he who denies them is not convinced or silenced by words. /

350   [I.1.A.f] As for the propositions containing their syllogisms, they are propositions in which assent is made only due to an intermediary. That intermediary is not among what escapes the mind – thus requiring the mind to seek it. Rather, whenever the two extreme terms of the problem are present to the mind, the intermediary is also present to it.[13] An example of this is our judgment that two is the half of four.

---

[12] Text: *imkānih* (its possibility).
[13] This is what Aristotle calls "quick wit." This faculty is said by Aristotle to see the major and minor terms and to grasp instantaneously the middle term which is the cause (Aristotle, *Anal. Post.*, I, 34, 10-16).

We have already exhausted the discussion of enumerating the types of propositions that must be accepted, grouped under beliefs, which in turn are grouped under admitted propositions.

[I.1.B] Among the widely-known propositions falling under this group,[14] there are [a] primary propositions and the like, classified as what must be accepted, not inasmuch as they must be accepted [in themselves], but inasmuch as they are generally acknowledged. /
351 And [b] opinions referred to as "praise-worthy," for which we may reserve the name "the widely-known" since they are based solely on notoriety.

These are opinions such that if the human being has his pure intellect, his estimative power and his senses free [from them; if] he is not educated to accept and acknowledge their judgments; [if] induction does not incline his strong opinion to make a judgment due to the multiplicity of particular cases; and [if] they are not called for by that which is in the human nature of mercy, abashment, pride, zeal, etc.; then the human being does not assert them due to abiding by his intellect, his estimative power or his sense. Examples are our judgments that stealing the wealth of others is an ugly act and that
352 lying is an ugly act which must not be pursued. / Of this genus [of acts], there is that which presents itself to the estimative power of many people – such as the ugly act of slaughtering animals – even though the Law turns many of them away from it, following the compassion of the instinct of them whose instinct is compassionate. These are the majority of people. Nothing of this is required by the pure intellect.

If a human being imagines himself as created at once with a complete intellect, without education and without abiding by the psychological and moral sentiments, he would not assert any such propositions. Rather, it would be possible for him to be ignorant of them and to stop short of [asserting] them. The case of his judgment that the whole is greater than the part is not the same. These widely-known propositions may be true and they may be false. If they are true, they are not related to the primary propositions and what resembles them, since the truth is not evident to the primordial intellect,[15] except by reflection and thought even though this intellect

---

[14] I.e., the group of beliefs.

[15] This is the natural intellect, or that which belongs to a human being at birth.

## CHAPTER 1

353 finds them praise-worthy. / But the true is other than the praise-worthy, as the false is other than the abominable. For the abominable may be true and the praise-worthy may be false.

Thus the widely-known propositions are concerned with either obligations, reformative education and those things on which divine laws agree, character and sentiments or inductive conclusions.

These propositions are presented either in an absolute manner or after the manner of skilled people or the leaders of a sect.

[I.1.C] The pure estimative propositions are false propositions. But the human estimative power asserts them in a very strong manner.
354 For the estimative power does not accept their contrary / or opposite, due to the fact that this power follows the senses, and what does not agree with the senses is not accepted by the estimative power. It is known that if the sensibles have principles and fundamentals, these principles and fundamentals must be prior to the sensibles. They are neither sensible, nor is their existence of the same sort as that of the sensible. Thus it is not possible to present that existence[16] in the estimative power.[17] For this reason, the estimative power itself and its acts cannot be represented in this power.[18] Because of this, the estimative power cannot assist the intellect in [grasping] the fundamentals which lead to the existence of these principles.[19] If the intellect and estimative power together pass to a conclusion, the estimative power retreats and refrains from accepting that whose necessity has been admitted.

This type of proposition is stronger in the soul than the widely-
355 known propositions which are not primary.[20] / They are almost like the primary propositions, and fall under the type of proposition that

---

[16] I.e., the existence of these principles and fundamentals.

[17] That is, since what is represented in the estimative power is only the sensible, and since these fundamentals and principles are not sensible but prior to the sensible, it follows that they cannot be represented in the estimative power.

[18] The assumption being that the estimative power and its acts are both non-sensible; and from what has been said, it follows that they cannot be represented in the estimative power.

[19] That is, since the material of the estimative power is only the sensible, and since the fundamentals together with the principles they produce are non-sensible, it follows that the estimative power cannot furnish the intellect with the assistance needed for the grasping of these fundamentals and principles.

[20] I.e., the praise-worthy opinions.

resembles the primary ones. These are judgments of the soul concerning things, prior to the sensibles, or more general than they, of the order of that which must not belong to them or of the order of that which must be believed to be in the sensibles.[21] Examples of this are the beliefs of him who holds that it is impossible not to have void at the limit of the plenum if the plenum is limited, and that it is impossible for any being to be such that one cannot point in the direction of its presence.[22]

Were these estimative propositions not opposed by the religious laws, they would have been widely-known. It is only through true religions and the philosophical sciences that the notoriety of these propositions is impeded. He who rejects that[23] can hardly struggle against himself for rejecting it, due to the stronghold that the estimative power has upon him. But if that which is rejected and not accepted by the estimative power is sensible, then it must be rejected and denied.[24] Yet even though it[25] is false and abominable, it is not without notoriety. The primary and estimative propositions which have no conflict with others[26] are of the widely-known type; but the converse is not true.

---

[21] Text: *aw'alā naḥū mā yajib an yakūn aw yuẓann fī al-maḥsūsāt* (or of the order of that which must be, or which is believed to be in the sensibles).

[22] I.e., every being is localized. But this is false. For God and the angels are not beings in the direction of whose presence one can point since they are non-spatial.

[23] *Wa-lā yakād al-madfū' 'an dhalik yaqāwim nafsahu fī daf' dhalik*. These are the propositions concerning the non-sensibles which are accepted by the intellect.

[24] Ibn Sīnā distinguishes here between two types of estimative propositions: the first is concerned with the non-sensible, and the second is concerned with the sensible. Since, as mentioned, the proper material of the estimative power is only the sensible, the first type of proposition must, therefore, be false; for the estimative power produces them by extending beyond its proper realm. However, their hold on the soul is so strong that they appear very similar to the primary propositions. As for the second type of estimative propositions, they are true since they are concerned with the proper material of the estimative power. That is why it is said that if the estimative power rejects anything sensible, that thing must be rejected. Similarly, it can be said that if the estimative power accepts a sensible, that sensible must be accepted.

This shows that what is stated at the outset of the discussion concerning estimative propositions (p. 353), namely that these propositions are false, is applicable only to the first type of estimative propositions mentioned here, and which Ibn Sīnā calls "purely estimative" – pure in the sense that their material is non-sensible.

[25] I.e., the first type of estimative propositions, mentioned in note 24.

[26] I.e., the second type of estimative propositions, mentioned in note 24.

## CHAPTER 1 125

Thus, we have ended [the discussion of] the various types of beliefs grouped under admitted propositions. /

356 [I.2] Propositions based on outside sources are either [A] received propositions or [B] determined propositions.

[I.2.A] Received propositions that are grouped under those which are based on outside sources are opinions adopted from a large or small number of scholars, or from a well-thought-of religious leader.

[I.2.B] Determined propositions are premises, adopted in accordance with the admission of the interlocutor, or are propositions whose acceptance and acknowledgement are necessary in the principles of the sciences – either with some denunciation (these are called "postulates") or with some tolerance and goodness of heart (these are called "posited principles"). Expect [a consideration of] these at a later point.[27] /

357 [II] Presumed propositions are statements and judgments which even though the arguer uses them decisively, he, nevertheless, follows nothing in himself except the dominant opinion without having the decisiveness of the intellect turned away from their opposite.

The widely-known propositions are a type of this group, according to the first and non-informed opinion. These are propositions that keep the mind restless, and thus preoccupy it from discerning the fact that they are [only] presumptions or that they are opposite the widely-known propositions, until [they are considered] for the second time.[28] Thus as if the soul submits to them when it first considers them. But if it goes back to itself,[29] that submission becomes a presumption or a falsification. /

358 By "presumption" here I mean an inclination of the soul with a feeling that the opposite is possible.[30] Among these premises, there is the statement of him who says, "Defend your brother, be he the wrong-doer or the one wronged."

---

[27] The Ninth Method, chapter 3.

[28] In other words, it takes more than one consideration to bring out the real nature of these propositions. A first consideration makes them appear as if they are not presumptions, but a kind of the widely-known propositions. It is only by further consideration that one can detect what they really are.

[29] That is, if the soul is freed from its restlessness and preoccupation.

[30] This is to be contrasted with the admitted propositions which, whether true or false, the soul is inclined to assert as true, and with no feeling that the opposite is possible.

The received propositions may fall under the presumed ones if the consideration is concerned with the aspect of the soul's inclination which occurs there with a feeling that the opposite is possible.[31]

[III] Ambiguous propositions that resemble others resemble something of the primary propositions, or of the widely-known propositions; but they are not these very propositions. / This resemblance is produced by either [1] the mediation of an expression, or [2] the mediation of a meaning.

[III.1] That which is produced by the mediation of an expression is such that the expression in the two [propositions] is the same, but the meaning is different.

[III.1.A] The meaning may be different in respect of the sense of the expression itself, as it is [in respect of] the comprehension of the expression "*al-'ayn.*"[32] However, this difference may be well-hidden, as in the case of "light" when it is sometimes taken in the sense of "sight" and sometimes in the sense of "truth in the intellect."

[III.1.B] Again, this difference in meaning may be in respect of that which occurs to the expression in its composition − / either in the composition itself of the expression, as in the phrase "*ghulām ḥasan*" with two *sukūns*,[33] or according to the diversity of signification of the connective particles in the composition which have no signification by themselves. Rather, it is only through the composition that these particles have signification. These particles are the instruments in their various types. Here is an example: "*mā ya'lam al-insān fa-huwa kamā ya'lamuh*" (what a human being knows is the same as what he knows; or a human being is what he knows as he knows it).

---

[31] That is, if one receives an idea from a scholar, a religious leader or any well-thought-of person, with a feeling that this idea is not necessarily true, then this idea is also classified under the genus of presumed propositions.

[32] Some of the senses in which "*al-'ayn*" is used are: "water fountain," "eye," "sun," "scalepan" and "dinar" (a Muslim gold coin minted at the end of the seventh century AD).

[33] A *sukūn* is a vowel-less sign, which when placed at the end of an expression indicates that that expression is case-free. But an expression of this sort is not governed by the rules of grammar, and hence its meaning is not determined. If, on the other hand, the phrase "*ghulām ḥasan*" does not have each of its words end with a *sukūn*, but is rather given in a case, then this phrase could mean "good boy" (if both words are in the nominative case), or "Ḥasan's boy" (if "*ghulām*" is in the nominative case and "*Ḥasan*" is in the genetive case).

Sometimes "*huwa*" (is) refers to "what is known" and sometimes to "human being."

[III.1.C] Further, the difference in meaning may be in accordance with what occurs to the expression in its declension. Or it may be produced in other ways, pointed out in different places, and which merit many lengthy elaborations. /

361 [III.2] As for the resemblance which is produced by [the mediation of] the meaning, it is something like [A] what is caused by imagining the converse. An example of this is taking "All snow is white" and believing "All white is snow."

[III.2.B] Similarly, if one takes the concomitant of a thing instead of that thing, then one believes that the judgment about the concomitant is about the thing. This is exemplified in the fact that [because] the human being has the concomitants of having estimation, being under obligation, and having speech, one imagines that anything that has some estimation and discernment is thus under obligation.

[III.2.C] Also, this is the case if a thing is described by that which occurs to it accidentally. An example of this is the judgment that scammony is refreshing, since in one respect it resembles what refreshes. The same is true of other things resembling these. /

362 In short, any proposition that pairs [with another] is[34] in a state which necessitates assent, since it resembles or is analogous to the proposition which is in that state, or is close to it.

Thus these are the propositions resembling others, either by expression or by meaning. What is left are the imagined propositions.

[IV] Imagined propositions are such that, when they are stated, they leave in the soul an astonishing effect of distress or pleasure. [Stating them] may strengthen the effect of the assent, and it may not be accompanied by assent. This is exemplified by the influence which our statement or judgment, "Honey is a vomited bile," has on the soul because of the fact that honey resembles bile, something which makes the soul reject honey and pull away from it. /

363 The majority of people proceed toward what they perform, and abstain from what they dispense with, in a manner produced by this type of movement of the soul and not in accordance with reflection or opinion.

---

[34] Text: *'alā annahu* (since it is).

Propositions involving assent – whether of the primary type and the like, or of the widely-known – may leave the same effects of moving or distressing the soul, and of having the soul approve their coming to it, as do imagined propositions. But they are primary and widely-known under one consideration, and imagined under another.[35]

It is not necessary that all imagined propositions be false, as it is not necessary that widely-known propositions and those that oppose the propositions which must be accepted[36] be inevitably false.

In short, a moving imagined statement depends on the element of astonishment which it produces either by [1] the goodness of its disposition, [2] the force of its truth, [3] the force of its notoriety, or [4] the goodness of its resemblance. But we reserve the name "imagined propositions" for those which leave an effect [on the soul] by resemblance. These may move the soul by dispositions external to assent.

## Chapter Two. A follow-up

We say that the name "admission" is said of the state of propositions, inasmuch as they are posited as principles[37] and give a judgment in just any manner.

Admission may be produced by the primordial intellect, by public agreement or by the just [opinion] of the opponent.

---

[35] That is, primary and widely-known propositions are such, inasmuch as the former is axiomatic and the latter is generally acknowledged. But if in addition to being what they are, these propositions move the soul either toward or away from something, then they are also imagined. However, to say that primary and widely-known propositions can become imagined is not to say that they become identical with the purely imagined propositions. For the basic character of the latter consists of moving the soul, while this is something added to the basic character of the former.

[36] I.e., the estimative propositions.

[37] *Waḍ'an*.

# The Seventh Method

### On Beginning the Second Composition[1] of Proof

*Chapter One. Remark: Concerning the syllogism, induction and analogy*

The types of proof for asserting something in which either [1] there can be no return to accepted and admitted propositions, or [2] such a return can be made but no return does take place,[2] are three: first the syllogism; second induction and what is of the same order; and third analogy and what is of the same order. /

Induction is a judgment about a universal, inasmuch as it is found in its many particulars. An example of this is our judgment: "Every animal moves its lower jaw during mastication." This is an induction from human beings, wild beasts and birds. / Induction does not necessarily lead to a correct science. For what has not been explored may be opposite what has been explored, such as the crocodile with respect to [the above-mentioned] example. Rather, that which differs [from the explored instances] may be the object sought,[3] in contrast to the judgment about all the rest.

Analogy is what is known by our contemporaries as *"qiyās."* [4] Analogy is an attempt to judge a thing by a judgment already made about a similar thing. It is a judgment about a particular thing, made

---

[1] I.e., the inductive, analogical or syllogistic argument – the first composition being the proposition.

[2] In proof, the premises are either immediate or underivable, or are the conclusions of premises that are immediate or underivable (*Tr. Log.*, p. 40). In the former case, one cannot go further in search of the acceptance of these premises. But in the latter case, one can go back to the immediate propositions on which the ones under consideration are based; however, this is not done (compare this with al-Fārābī, *Short Commentary*, p. 59).

[3] Text: *wal-maṭlūb* (and the object sought).

[4] This is the term Ibn Sīnā uses for "syllogism." The term he uses for "analogy" is *"tamthīl."*

by virtue of a similar one concerning another particular thing with
369 which the former agrees by a common idea. / Our contemporaries
called that about which the judgment is made "branch,"[5] that which
resembles it "fundamental"[6] and that which is common to the two
"idea" or "cause."[7] But this too is weak.[8] What insures the analogy is
that the common idea is the cause or sign for the judgment about
what is called "fundamental." /

370 As for the syllogism, it is the underpinning [of the proof]. The
syllogism is a discourse composed of statements. If the propositions
which the syllogism involves are admitted,[9] this by itself necessarily
leads to another statement. /

372 If the propositions are given in something like what is called
"syllogism," "induction" or "analogy," then they are called "premises." A premise, therefore, is a proposition which has become a part
of a syllogism or [of another type of] proof.

The essential parts of what is called "premise," which are the
remainders after the analysis to primary single elements and which
are the smallest parts of which the proposition is composed, are called
373 "terms."[10] / Here is an example: "Every C is B; every B is A; from
this it follows that every C is A."[11] Each of our statements, "Every C
is B" and "Every B is A," is a premise. C, B and A are terms. The

---

[5] *Far'an.*

[6] *Aṣlan.*

[7] *Ma'nan wa-'illa.*

[8] That is, like induction, analogy is a weak form of proof. In fact it is considered by Ibn Sīnā to be the weakest form of proof, since its subject is an individual; and as mentioned, only arguments with universal subjects must be employed in the sciences (see Introduction, p. 15).

[9] Even though it is true to say that if the propositions contained in the syllogism are admitted, they necessarily lead to another proposition, Ibn Sīnā makes clear (*Ish.*, Part I, p. 373) that it is not a condition of the syllogism that its propositions be admitted. Rather, its condition is that if its propositions are laid down, even by somebody who does not believe they are true, another proposition necessarily follows.

[10] *Ḥudūdan.* The other meaning of "*ḥudūd*" is "limits," from which, we assume, it has also come to mean "definitions" – since the limits of a thing give the determination of that thing. Compare this definition of "terms" with that of Aristotle: "I call that a term into which the premiss is resolved, i.e., both the predicate and that of which it is predicated, 'being' being added and 'not being' removed, or vice versa." (*Anal. Pr.*, I, 1, 24b, 16-18).

[11] Islamic logicians place the minor premise before the major one.

statement, "Every C is A," is a conclusion. And what is composed of two premises, in the manner just illustrated, so that it necessarily leads to this conclusion, is the syllogism.[12]

It is not a condition of [this kind of proof] to have admitted propositions in order that it be a syllogism. Rather, its condition is such that, if its propositions are admitted, then another statement necessarily follows from them. This is the condition for its being a syllogism.[13] But its premises may need not be admitted, yet the discourse remains a syllogism because it is such that, if what it contains is admitted as not necessary, still another statement necessarily follows from it.

374   *Chapter Two. Remark: Concerning specifically the syllogism*

The syllogism, as has been determined by us, is of two kinds, [1] conjunctive[14] and [2] repetitive.[15]

---

[12] "Syllogism" is used by Ibn Sīnā in two senses: (1) in the sense of the premises and the conclusion of this kind of proof, and (2) in the sense of the conjunction of the premises alone. That Ibn Sīnā here uses "syllogism" in the second sense is evident throughout the present method (see, for example, p. 379).

[13] The same condition for the nature of the syllogism had already been given by Aristotle: "A syllogism is discourse in which, certain things being stated, something other than what is stated follows of necessity from their being so." (*Anal. Pr.*, I, 1, 24b, 18-20).

[14] *Iqtirānī*.

[15] *Istithnā'ī*. This term has caused translators great difficulty. Some have translated it as "exceptive" (see, for example, I. Madkour, *L'Organon d'Aristote dans le monde arabe* [Paris: Vrin, 1934], p. 203; and *The Propositional Logic of Avicenna*, trans. N. Shehaby [Dordrecht, Boston, 1973], p. 5) or as "exclusion" (al-Fārābī, *Short Commentary*, trans. Rescher, pp. 75ff.). This is the literal meaning. But this translation has often rendered the original text either very hard to understand, or in some cases senseless. The following is an example of this.

"Every disjunctive conditional [syllogism] whose alternatives are complete [is such that] when either one of them [viz., the two alternatives] is 'excluded', the conclusion agrees with the opposite of the other alternative; and if the opposite of either one of them is 'excluded', then this yields the other alternative itself." (al-Fārābī, *Short Commentary*, trans. Rescher, p. 78).

Others, such as Goichon, have rendered it as "hypothetical" (*Dir. Rem.*, p. 194). But first, not all repetitive syllogisms are hypothetical; some are disjunctive (see the Eighth Method, Chapter 3). Second, this name has nothing to do with the name "*istithnā'ī*," given to this kind of syllogism by Ibn Sīnā. And third, Ibn Sīnā is at pains

[1] The conjuctive syllogism is one in which there is no explicit mention of either one of the extreme contradictories, incorporating the conclusion. Rather, it has this in potentiality only[16] as the above-mentioned example shows.[17]

[2] As for the repetitive syllogism, it is one in which there is an explicit mention of that. / This is exemplified in saying, "If 'Abd al-Lāh is rich, he is not unjust; but he is rich, therefore, he is not unjust." Thus, you find in [this] syllogism [an explicit mention of] one of the two extreme contradictories, incorporating the conclusion – this is the conclusion itself.[18] Another example of the repetitive syllogism is, "If this fever is the fever of a day, it does not produce a great change in pulse; but it has produced a great change in pulse, it follows that it is not the fever of a day." Again you find in [this] syllogism [an explicit mention of] one of the two extreme contradictories, incorporating the conclusion – this is the contradictory of the conclusion.[19]

---

to show that conditional syllogisms, some of which are hypothetical, can be conjunctive (*Ish.*, Part I, p. 375). In fact, he is quite critical of those who fail to understand that both predicative and conditional syllogisms can be conjunctive. Thus, even though some hypothetical syllogisms are repetitive, it is not because they are hypothetical that they are such. By now it should be clear why translating "*istithnā'ī*" as "hypothetical" is highly misleading. It is also interesting to note that Goichon translates "*mustathnā*" (the minor premise which is a repetition of one element in the major) as "*choisie*" (chosen) (p. 194, note 6).

In his article, "The Term *Istithnā'* in Arabic Logic," Kwame Gyekye says: "We should recall an earlier statement that 'repetition' used in the Hebrew translation for *istithnā'*, namely *hishshanuth*, reflects the root of the Arabic word *th-n-y* ... means: 'to repeat,' 'to do twice' (Wehr). We know, of course, that the minor premise (i.e., the additional assumption: *prolepsis, prosthesis, al-mus-tathnāt*) is a repetition of one part of the major premise." (*Journal of the American Oriental Society*, 92 [January-March 1972], 82-92).

Following Gyekye's interpretation, which seems most reasonable, we have translated "*istithnā'ī*" as "repetitive syllogism."

[16] In other words, it is one in which there is no actual mention either of the conclusion or of its contradictory.

[17] I.e., the example given on p. 373.

[18] I.e., "He is not unjust" whose contradictory is "He is just."

[19] I.e., "This fever is the fever of a day." The last two examples are of the same type of repetitive syllogism, namely that which includes a connective conditional proposition. This type, as well as others, together with the rules for their validity, will be discussed in the Eighth Method, Chapter 3.

Conjuctive syllogisms may consist of simple predicative propositions, simple conditional propositions, or they may be composed of the two. Those which consist of simple conditionals may be formed of simple connective propositions, simple disjunctive propositions, or they may be composed of the two. As for the majority of logicians, they have paid attention to predicative syllogisms only, thinking that conditional syllogisms can only be repetitive.

We will mention predicative syllogisms with their various types.
376 / This will be followed by [a discussion of] some conditional conjunctive syllogisms, which are most used, and which have the strongest hold on our natures. After that we will [treat] repetitive syllogism. And finally we will mention some states which the syllogisms undergoes, and the syllogism by contradiction. We will limit ourselves in this summary to this much.

377 *Chapter Three. Remark: Concerning specifically the conjunctive syllogism*

In the conjunctive syllogism, you find a repeated common thing which is called "middle term," such as B in the preceding example.[20] In it you also find something proper to each of the two premises, such as C in one of the premises of our example, and A in the other premise. And you find the conclusion, obtained only by the union of these two extreme terms, where we said, "... from this it follows that
378 every C is A." / What becomes the subject of the conclusion or the antecedent, such as C in our example, is called "minor term." And what becomes the predicate of the conclusion or the consequent, such as A in our example, is called "major term."

The premise which has the minor term is called "minor premise." /
379 The premise which has the major term is called "major premise." And the composition of both is called "conjunction." The form of composition according to the manner of positing the middle term in relation to the two extreme terms is called "figure." And the conjunction which yields a conclusion is called "syllogism."

---

[20] I.e., the example mentioned on p. 373.

384 *Chapter Four. Remark: Concerning the various types of predicative conjunctive syllogisms*

The divisions [of this type of syllogism] require that the middle term be either: [1] a predicate of the minor premise and a subject of the major one, [2] the converse of this,[21] [3] a predicate of both the minor and the major premises, or [4] a subject of both of them. /

385 As the first division, called "the first figure," had been found perfect with much goodness – inasmuch as its syllogistic character, i.e., the necessity[22] of yielding a conclusion, is evident in itself and not in need of a proof[23] – the converse of this division has been found remote from our nature.[24] Giving evidence for its syllogistic character, i.e., [the necessity of] drawing a conclusion from it, requires a doubly-hard effort.[25] And its syllogistic character does not present itself to the mind and nature.[26] /

386 As for the other two divisions, even though their syllogistic character is not evident, they are of the syllogisms that are within the reach of our nature. The normal nature can grasp their syllogistic character before evidence for that is given. Or the evidence for that is presented to the mind by the mind itself, and thus the reason for their being syllogisms is closely attended to. That is why these two divisions became accepted, while the converse of the first one had

---

[21] This figure has become known as Galen's fourth figure. But whether Galen was the first to admit it still remains a matter of controversy.

[22] Text: *ḍarūriyya* (necessary).

[23] For Ibn Sīnā, the perfection and the imperfection of syllogisms require the same conditions posited by Aristotle before: "I call that a perfect syllogism which needs nothing other than what has been stated to make plain what necessarily follows; a syllogism is imperfect if it needs either one or more propositions which are indeed the necessary consequences of the terms set down, but have not been expressly stated as premises" (*Anal. Pr.*, I, 1, 24b, 22-24).

[24] *Ba'īdan 'an aṭ-ṭab'*; in the sense that its syllogistic character is not grasped by the mind directly.

[25] The third and fourth figures are reduced to the first, which is the only perfect figure, by conversion of one of the premises. But in order to reduce the second figure to the first, both premises must be converted. This is what is meant by saying, "... requires a doubly-hard effort."

[26] That is why the figure in which the middle term is a subject of the minor premise and a predicate of the major one is admitted by Ibn Sīnā, but is cast aside as not worthy of consideration.

been rejected. Thus the figures of the predicative conjunctive syllogism that are recognized became three in number.

In these three figures, no conclusion can be drawn from two particular propositions. As to whether [a conclusion can be drawn] from two negative propositions, a consideration of this will be presented to you later on.[27]

387         *[Chapter Five]. The first figure*

In order for this figure to be a syllogism whose conjunction leads to a conclusion, it must [1] meet the condition of having a minor premise which is affirmative or of the same order as the affirmative. If it is possible or concrete, it is true in affirmation as it is true in negation. / 
388 And its minor term is subsumed under the middle one. [2] Also its major premise must be universal so that its judgment could be carried over to the minor term since it is common to all that is subsumed under the middle term.

That the syllogistic conjunctions of this figure lead to conclusions is 
389 evident. / Thus if "Every C is B" and then you say, "Every B is, by necessity or otherwise, A," it follows that "Every C is also A"[28] – [with the conclusion having] that mode.[29]

390 Similarly, if you say, / "By necessity, or otherwise, nothing of B is A," then no doubt the judgment is carried over to C.[30] Again, if you say, "Some C is B," and then you impose on B any kind of judgment – be that negative or affirmative – after being common to every

---

[27] Ibn Sīnā's reponse is "Yes, if one of the negative premises implies an affirmative one" (see p. 396 of the present method).

[28] The first syllogism of the first figure is AAA (Barbara):

    (m):    All C is B
    (M):    All B is A

    (C):    All C is A

[29] I.e., that of the major premise, be it necessity or any other mode.

[30] This is the second syllogism of the first figure: EAE (Celarent):

    (m):    All C is B
    (M)    No B is A

    (C):    No C is A

B, then this judgment is carried over to this some of C which is B.[31] Thus the syllogistic conjunctions of this first figure are these four; that is, if every C is, in some manner of being, B in actuality. /

391　But if every C is B in possibility, then the judgment must not be carried over from B to C in an evident manner. However, if the judgment about B is in possibility, then there is a possibility of a possibility which is close to being known by the mind as a possibility. For it is within the reach of our nature to judge that the possible of a possible is possible. /

392　If every C is B according to the real and proper possibility, and if every B is A absolutely, then it is permissible that every C is A in actuality, and it is permissible that it is so in potentiality. And what is common to both must be the possible, in the general sense. /

393　If every B is A by necessity, then the truth is that the conclusion is
394　necessary. / To show this, let us sight a close aspect. Thus we say, "Because if C becomes B, it is then judged as necessarily having A for a predicate." This means that A cannot be removed [as the predicate] of C, as long as the essence of C exists; and not that it cannot be removed as long as C is B only. If C is judged as A when it is B only
395　and not when it is not B, then the statement, / "Every B is by necessity A," is false, as you know. Because what it means is that everything described as B, always or not always, is described by necessity as A as long as its essence exists, be it B or not. /

396　If the minor premise is possible or absolute and the negative is true with it, then it is permissible for it to be negative and to produce a conclusion. Because what negates the real possible implies what affirms it.

Thus the conclusions of the syllogism of this figure follow in every case,[32] in their quality and mode, the major premise, except if the

---

[31] The third and fourth syllogisms of this figure are, respectively, as follows:

| AII (Darii): | (m): | Some C is B |
|---|---|---|
|  | (M): | All B is A |
|  | (C): | Some C is A |
| EIO (Ferio): | (m): | Some C is B |
|  | (M): | No B is A |
|  | (C): | Some C is not A |

[32] Text: *mawḍi'* (place).

397 minor premise is possible, in the proper sense, and the major concrete – then the conclusion is possible, in the proper sense – / or if the minor premise is affirmative and necessary and the major absolute, in the general sense[33] – then the conclusion is affirmative and necessary, except in a case which will be mentioned later.[34]

Do not pay attention to what is said, namely that the conclusion follows the inferior of the two premises in every thing,[35] but in quality and quantity [only],[36] with the exception that has been mentioned. /

399 You must know that if the minor premise is necessary and the major purely concrete, belonging to the genus of the concrete, in the sense that as long as the subject is qualified by that with which it is qualified, no syllogism with true premises is formed. For the major
400 premise is false, since if we say, / "Every C is by necessity B," and then say, "Every B is qualified as A, as long as it is qualified as B, and not always," we judge that all that which is qualified as B is qualified thus, only at a certain time, and not always. This is opposite the minor premise. Rather, the major premise must be more general than
401 this[37] and than the necessary one, / in order for it to be true. But then the conclusion is necessary, and does not follow the major premise. /
402 This, too, is an exception.[38] It is necessary only because C endures as B, thus enduring by necessity as A.

403 *Chapter Six. Remark: Concerning the second figure*

You must know that the truth regarding the second figure is that in it there is no syllogism constituted of two absolute propositions with
404 common application, of two possible propositions, / or of a mixture of both. Further, there is no doubt that in it there is no syllogism

---

[33] Text: *aw aṣ-ṣughrā muṭlaqa khāṣṣa sāliba wal-kubrā muwjiba ḍarūriyya* (or the minor absolute, in the particular sense, and negative; and the major affirmative and necessary).
[34] See pp. 399-402 of the present method.
[35] I.e., in quantity, quality and mode.
[36] I.e., not in mode.
[37] I.e., than the purely concrete.
[38] This is the third of the exceptions (promised us p. 397) to the rule that the conclusion follows, in its quality and mode, the major premise. The other two exceptions were mentioned on pp. 396-397.

consisting of two affirmative, or two negative absolute propositions, or of two possible propositions, in whatever manner.

First, the disagreement is concerned with the two absolute propositions only. The commoners believe that if they differ in negation and affirmation, a syllogism, therefore, may be formed of them. But our view is different. / [Second], concerning the pure absolute propositions and the possible ones, the disagreement is the same. In the second figure, there is no syllogism constituted of them according to us. That is, because one thing or rather two things, of which one is the predicate of the other, may have something predicated of one of them or of both in an absolute affirmation or[39] negated in an absolute negation. And it may be affirmed and negated at the same time of every individual falling under one [of the two] concepts, or of the individuals of the two things of which one is predicated of the other. Nothing of this requires that the thing be negated of itself / or that one of the two things be negated of the other. All of this may occur to the two things, of which one is negated of the other, without requiring that one of the two be a predicate of the other. From what has preceded, it follows that neither negation nor affirmation is attained. And thus no conclusion can be drawn. / What is used by them as a proof for drawing a conclusion from two absolute propositions, different in quality and of which the major premise is universal, is something that will be mentioned later. There is discontinuity between propositions that are absolute, in a general sense, and those that are concrete, in a general sense. What one can rely on [for demonstrating the second figure] is either conversion, and neither of them converts in negation, or contradiction, by employing a contradictory. But the conditions of a contradictory are not applicable to these propositions. /

Rather, in this figure syllogisms are formed of absolute premises, of which one is affirmative and the other negative, only if the negative premise meets the condition of converting, or of having a contradictory of its type. You know which negative absolute propositions are such.

Thus if there is here a composition of two absolute propositions, of two necessary ones, or of an absolute proposition, with common

---

[39] Text: *wa* (and).

## CHAPTER 6

409 application, and a necessary one, / the condition is that the two propositions differ in quality – the major premise being universal – and the judgment is of the mode of the converted negative proposition.

The first mood of the second figure is something like the phrase, "Every C is B, nothing of A is B, therefore, nothing of C is A." [40] /
410 Since we convert the major, making it "Nothing of B is A," and then add to it the minor premise, thus forming the second mood of the first figure. The conclusion[41] is of the mode of the major premise.

The second mood of this figure is something like the phrase, "Nothing of C is B, every A is B, therefore, nothing of C is A." [42] /
411 Since we convert the minor premise, we then conclude, "Nothing of A is C." After that we convert the conclusion. Also the conclusion[43] takes the mode of the negative [premise]. If it is an absolute proposition, that to which it is converted is also absolute.

The third mood of the present figure is like the phrase, "Some C is B, nothing of A is B, therefore, some C is not A." [44] Find evidence for this from what you already know.[45]

---

[40] The first syllogism of the second figure is: EAE (Cesare):

| | | |
|---|---|---|
| (m): | All C is B | |
| (M): | No A is B | |

(C): No C is A

By converting the major, this syllogism is reduced to the second syllogism of the first figure (Celarent).

[41] *Al-'ibra*.

[42] The second syllogism of the second figure is: AEE (Camestres):

| | | |
|---|---|---|
| (m): | No C is B | |
| (M): | All A is B | |

(C): No C is A

By converting the minor and the conclusion, this syllogism is also reduced to the second syllogism of the first figure (Celarent).

[43] *Al-'ibra*.

[44] The third syllogism of the second figure is: EIO (Festino):

| | | |
|---|---|---|
| (m) | Some C is B | |
| (M): | No A is B | |

(C): Some C is not A

[45] Convert the major and you get the fourth syllogism of the first figure: EIO (Ferio).

412    The fourth mood is like the phrase, "Some C is not B, every A is not B, / therefore, some C is not A." [46] Or else, "Every C is A, and every A has been B, therefore every C is B." But it has been stated that, "Some C is not B." This is contradictory.

But for this, there is evidence other than by contradiction. Let D be the some which is of C which is not B, the nothing of D is B, and [since] every A is B, therefore, nothing of D is A. But some C is D, and
413    nothing of D is A; therefore, not every C is A. / From this, you know that the conclusion[47] takes the mode of the negative [premise]. It is not possible to demonstrate this mood by conversion. Because the minor premise is a particular negative proposition, and, therefore, does not convert; and the major premise converts to a particular proposition; thus no syllogism can be formed from its conjunction with the minor one. This is so because no syllogism is formed of two particular propositions.

In addition to all of this, there is no possible proposition among the premises. If there is a mixture of a possible proposition and an absolute one, of the genus which does not convert, then what has preceded concerning the prevention of the construction of a syllogism from two absolute propositions of such a genus shows clearly the prevention of the construction of a syllogism from this mixture. But if it is of the genus which we are using now, and the absolute [premise]
414    is negative, / then a syllogism may be constructed, if the conditions are satisfied; if the major premise is a negative universal, of the type of absolute previously-mentioned, and the possible one affirmative or negative, then [this syllogism] is reduced to the first figure by conversion or by hypothesis – thus yielding a conclusion. And the conclusion is that which you have known in the first figure. /
415    However, if the major premise is not negative, but affirmative, then there is no syllogism except in [a manner requiring] detailed [explication] for which there is no need here. /
420    To this you must compare the mixture of the necessary proposition with another if it is of this form – after you learn that in this mixture,

---

[46] The fourth syllogism of the second figure is: AOO (Baroko):

(m):   Some C is not B
(M):   All A is B

---

(C):   Some C is not A

[47] *Al-'ibra*.

CHAPTER 7     141

there is an increase in the number of syllogisms. That is, if the composition is of a pure possible proposition and a pure necessary one, / or of a pure concrete proposition and a pure necessary one – and the major premise is universal – then the syllogism is complete, whether the two propositions are both affirmative, or both negative, let alone [if] they are different. As for if they differ, when the major premise is universal, this you must know from what you have already learned.

But if they agree, you know that if C is such that B is only true of the whole if it is a non-necessary affirmation, then B is [true] of everything which is C, or of what is assumed to be a part of C, without necessity. A is the opposite of C, when B is [true] of all that which is A by necessity. Thus it is known that the nature of C, or what is assumed to be a part of it, is different from that of A; and neither of them is included in the other. This is not possible, whether, after this difference, there is agreement in the affirmative quality or in the negative quality. / The same is true of the some of C which is different from A in that [way] – if the minor premise is particular. You must know that the conclusion is always necessarily negative. This is among what they did not pay attention to.

*Chapter Seven. Remark: Concerning the third figure*

For the conjunctions of this figure to give a conclusion, they must satisfy the conditions of / having the minor premise affirmative or of the same order as the affirmative, as you have learned, and of having a universal proposition, regardless of which one that is. You know that the conjunctions of this figure are, then, six in number.

But the six have this in common: that their conclusions must be particular propositions only, and they must not involve a universal proposition. Thus if you say, "Every human being is an animal," and "Every human being is rational," it does not follow that every animal is rational but that some animals are rational – by converting the minor premise. Make this, then, as a standard for yourself / in [the syllogisms] that are composed of two universal propositions.

But if the major premise is a particular proposition, then you do not benefit from the conversion of the minor one. For if it is converted, it becomes a particular. Then if you join it to the other particular, the conjunction would be of two particular propositions, and thus it does not yield a conclusion. Rather, you must convert the major premise and then the conclusion, as you have learned. You must know that the conclusion[48] retains the mode of the major premise only, as has been[49] determined in the first figure, along the lines described. /

426   The syllogism which is demonstrated by the conversion of its minor premise is clear. As for the syllogism which is demonstrated by the conversion of its major premise, that is shown by hypothesis.

427   Suppose that some B which is A is D. Then / "Every D is A." Thus you say, "Every D is B." But "Every B is C." Hence, "Every D is C." This is joined to "Every D is A." It follows that "Some C is A." The mode [of the conclusion] is that which is necessitated by the mode of our statement, "Every D is A," which is the mode of "Some B is A." /

428   Those who attribute the judgment to the mode of the minor premise believe that the minor becomes the major at the conversion of the latter, and thus the judgment would be for its mode. Then it is converted. And the mode after the conversion is that of the original. But they err, just because they believe that the conversion preserves the mode. You already know their error.

There remains the syllogism which is not demonstrated by conversion. This is one in which the major premise is a negative particular proposition – thus it does not convert – and the minor

429   converts to a particular. / Hence no syllogism can be formed. This is demonstrated only by way of contradiction or by way of hypothesis.

The way of contradiction is to say, "If it is not the case that some C is not A, then every C is A." But every B has been C. It follows that "Every B is A." Yet it has been stated that "Every B is not A." This is contradictory.

And the way of hypothesis is to say, "Let the some which is B, and not A, be D." Then nothing of D is A. From there, you yourself complete [this], and also consider the mode [of the conclusion] which is necessitated by the major premise. /

430   Thus the conjunctions of the third figure are six: [A] of two affirmative universal propositions;[50] [B] of two affirmative proposi-

---

[48] *Al-'ibra*.
[49] Text: *wa-hiya al-latī* (is what is).
[50] The first syllogism of the third figure is: AAI (Darapti):

(m):   All C is B
(M):   All C is A

---

(C):   Some B is A

tions, the minor being particular;[51] [C] of two affirmative propositions, the major being particular;[52] [D] of two universal propositions, the major being negative;[53] [E] of an affirmative particular as the minor premise, and a universal negative as the major one;[54] [F] of an affirmative universal as the minor premise, and a negative particular as the major.[55] These [conjunctions] are mentioned as five. But God is most knowing of what is correct.

---

Converting the minor premise by limitation, this syllogism is reduced to the third syllogism of the first figure AII (Darii).

[51] The second syllogism of the third figure is: AII (Datisi):

(m): Some C is B
(M): All C is A

---

(C): Some B is A

Through conversion by limitation of the minor premise, this syllogism is reduced to the third syllogism of the first figure: AII (Darii).

[52] The third syllogism of the present figure is: IAI (Disamis):

(m): All C is B
(M): Some C is A

---

(C): Some B is A

By converting the major premise and the conclusion, the present syllogism is reduced to the third syllogism of the first figure: AII (Darii).

[53] The fourth syllogism of the third figure is: EAO (Felapton):

(m): All C is B
(M): No C is A

---

(C): Some B is not A

Through conversion by limitation of the minor premise, the present syllogism is reduced to the fourth syllogism of the first figure: EIO (Ferio).

[54] The fifth syllogism of the third figure is: EIO (Ferison):

(m): Some C is B
(M): No C is A

---

(C): Some B is not A

Converting the minor premise, this syllogism is reduced to the fourth syllogism of the first figure: EIO (Ferio).

[55] The sixth syllogism of the third figure is: OAO (Bokardo):

(m): All C is B
(M): Some C is not A

---

(C): Some B is not A

While (A) to (E) are demonstrated by conversion, (F) is demonstrated by way of contradiction or by way of hypothesis.

# The Eighth Method

### ON CONDITIONAL SYLLOGISMS, AND ON WHAT FOLLOWS THE SYLLOGISM

*Chapter One. Remark: Concerning conditional conjunctive syllogisms*

We will mention some of these syllogisms, leaving aside those of them which are not grasped by us naturally,[1] after having treated all of them sufficiently in *ash-Shifā'* and in other works of ours. /

We say that of the conditional conjunctive syllogisms[2] three figures may be formed. These are similar to the figures of the predicative syllogisms. They have in common a consequent / or an antecedent, and they differ in a consequent or an antecedent as do the figures of the predicative syllogisms; the latter has in common a subject or a predicate, and they differ in a subject or a predicate. Also the rules [governing these figures] are the same as those [governing the predicative ones]. / The community [of an element] may occur between a predicative proposition and a disjunctive one, as in your saying, "Two is a number; and every number is either even, or it is odd." From what has preceded, it is easy to infer the rules for this.

Also a disjunctive proposition and a predicative one may have [an element] in common, as your saying in this sense, "Let / A be either B, C or D; and every B, C and D is E; therefore, every A is E." From what has preceded, it is also easy to infer the rules for this. /

Further, a conjunction may be formed of a connective conditional proposition and a predicative one. Of this the easiest to grasp naturally[3] is [that in which] the predicative proposition shares the consequent with the affirmative connective conditional, in one of the manners in which the predicative propositions share [the predicate].

---

[1] Text: *lais qarīban min aṭ-ṭab'* (what is not close to the nature).
[2] *Al-muttaṣilāt*. This is the same term used for "connective conditional."
[3] Text: *aqrab mā yakūn min dhalik ilā aṭ-ṭab'* (what is closest to the nature).

But the conclusion, then, is a connective conditional whose antecedent is that antecedent itself, and whose consequent is the conclusion of the composition of the consequent which was conjoined in the predicative proposition. An example of this is "If A is B, / then every C is D, and every D is E." It follows from this that "If A is B, then every C is E." It is for you to enumerate the rest of the divisions from what you already know. /

Such a composition[4] may be of two connective conditional propositions, each of which shares the consequent of the other, if that consequent is also a connective; / and its syllogism is the same as that.

A complete discussion of conditional connective syllogisms is not appropriate in a summary like this.

*Chapter Two. Remark: Concerning the syllogism of equals*[5]

Some things concerning the judgments of the premises may be known, yet left out. And the syllogism is built in a form different from [that of the perfect] syllogism. An example of this is "C is equal to B, and B is equal to A; therefore, C is equal to A." But "what is equal to some thing, which is equal to another, is equal to that other"[6] has been left out of this. In the syllogism, certain aspects that require community in the whole of the middle term are substituted for the community in a part of it.

*Chapter Three. Remark: Concerning repetitive conditional syllogisms*

Repetitive conditional syllogisms are either:

[1] one in which there is a connective conditional, and what is repeated is either [A] its antecedent itself, thus giving the consequent itself as a conclusion. An example of this is "If the sun is out, then the stars are hidden; / but the sun is out, therefore, the stars are hidden." Or [B] the contradictory of its consequent, thus giving the contradictory of the antecedent as a conclusion. An example of this is saying, "... but the stars are not hidden." Thus the conclusion is

---

[4] I.e., the composition which is easiest to grasp.

[5] This is one kind of relational syllogism, and what is stated about it is applicable to the other kinds of relational syllogisms, such as that of resemblance.

[6] Text: *musāwī al-musāwī musāwī* (an equal is an equal to an equal).

"Therefore, the sun is not out." Nothing other than this is concluded. /

450 [2] Another in which there is a real disjunctive proposition, and what is repeated is either [A] whichever [part][7] of the disjunctive, thus giving the contradictory of the other parts as a conclusion. An example of this is "This number is either complete, excessive or deficient; but it is complete." Thus the conclusion is the contradictory of the remaining [parts]. Or [B] what is repeated is the contradictory of which ever [part] of the disjunctive, thus giving what remains itself – be that one or more [parts] – as a conclusion. An example of this is "... but it is not complete, therefore, it is either excessive or deficient," [and so on], until the repeatable elements are exhausted. There remains one division.

[3] Or one in which there is a non-real disjunctive proposition, /
451 which is either [A] preventive of exclusion only. Repeating the contradictory [or a part] gives the other part itself as a conclusion.[8] Here is an example: "Either Zayd is in water, or he is not drowned; but he is drowned, therefore he is in water." [Or] "... he is not in water; therefore, he is not drowned." Another example is "Either this is not an animal, or this is not a plant; but it is an animal; therefore, it is not a plant." Or "... it is a plant; therefore, it is not an animal." Or

[3B]. The disjunctive proposition is of the genus which is intended to prevent the union [of the parts] only, but it permits the elimination [of all the parts] together. A group of people have called it "the incomplete disjunction or conflict." Thus repeating [a part] of it yields
452 only the contradictory of / the rest.[9] This is exemplified in your

---

[7] Text: *'ayn mā yattafiq* (whichever [part] itself). "Itself" has been deleted since it adds nothing.

[8] Text: *fa-lā yantuj illā istithnā' an-naqīḍ li-'ayn al-ākhar* (nothing is concluded except the repetition of the contradictory of the other [part] itself).

[9] Text: *fa-ḥīna'idhn innamā yantuj fīhā istithnā' al-'ayn wa-takūn an-natīja naqīḍ al-tālī fa-qaṭ* (thus repeating in it [a part] itself only, then the conclusion is [in another variation not chosen by Dunyā, "and the conclusion is" is left out] the contradictory of the consequent [in another variation, also not chosen by Dunyā, "the consequent" is replaced by "the rest"] only ["only" is eliminated in another variation]). It is clear that Dunyā shows no understanding of this passage, nor does Goichon fare any better. Here is how she renders it: "... [tel est le cas] lorsque le choix de l'œil est le seul à amener une conclusion, et celle-ci est le contraire du conséquent, uniquement" (Goichon, *Dir. Rem.*, p. 220).

saying, "Either this is an animal, or it is a tree," in answering him who says, "This is an animal, [and] this is a tree." [10]

453 *Chapter Four. Remark: Concerning the syllogism by contradiction*

The syllogism by contradiction is composed of two syllogisms, one of which is conjunctive and the other repetitive. An example of this is "If it is not the case that our statement, 'Every C is not B,' is true, then 454 our statement, 'Every C is B,' is true." / But every B is D, which is an evident premise, concerning which there is no doubt or which was made evident by a syllogism. The conclusion that is drawn from this is "If it is not the case that our statement, 'Every C is not B,' is true, then it is the case that every C is D." Then we take this conclusion and we repeat the contradictory of the impossible, i.e., the consequent. Thus we say, "But every C is not D." The conclusion is, then, the contradictory of the antecedent which is "(not) it is not the case that our statement, 'Every C is not B,' is true." /

457 As for how the predicative direct syllogism leads to [the syllogism] by contradiction, and how the latter leads to the former, this is [a subject] for another investigation which treats of the state of the conjunction between the consequent and the predicative proposition.
458 / But for that, there is no need at the present. It turns on taking the contradictory of the impossible conclusion and joining it to the true premise, concerning which there is no doubt, thus giving the impossible antecedent as it is, as a conclusion.

---

[10] A completion of this syllogism is either "... this is an animal; therefore, it is not a tree," or "... this is a tree; therefore, it is not an animal."

# The Ninth Method

### In Which a Brief Explication of the Demonstrative Sciences Is Given[1]

*Chapter One. Remark: Concerning the various types of syllogisms, with respect to their matters and their production of assent*

Demonstrative syllogisms are composed of premises that must be accepted. If these premises are necessary, the conclusion drawn from them is necessary, in the manner of their necessity;[2] / and [if] they are possible, the conclusion drawn from them is possible.

Dialectical syllogisms are composed of widely-known propositions and determined ones,[3] be they necessary, possible or impossible.

Rhetorical syllogisms are composed of presumed propositions, received ones, which are not widely-known, and those resembling them, be they what they are, even if impossible. /

Poetical syllogisms are composed of imagined propositions, inasmuch as their imagined aspect is considered, be they true or false. In short, they are composed of premises, inasmuch as these premises have a certain disposition and composition, which the soul receives by virtue of their resemblance or by virtue of their truth. [That is, as long as] there is nothing to prevent this [reception]. And meter enhances this [reception].

---

[1] A demonstration is a syllogism with a certain (*yaqīniyya*) conclusion drawn from certain premises (*Naj.*, p. 66).

[2] Recall the various types of necessity, elaborated in the Fourth Method, Chapter Three. If the necessity of the premises of a demonstration is unconditioned or absolute, then the necessity of the conclusion is the same. And if the necessity of the premises is conditioned whether by the existence of the essence or otherwise, then the necessity of the conclusion is of the same type.

[3] As you may recall, there are, according to Ibn Sīnā, two kinds of determined propositions: that which is determined by the interlocutor, and that which is employed in the sciences (p. 356). Since dialectical syllogisms are not scientific, it must be the case that the former kind of determined propositions is intended here.

## CHAPTER 1

463    Do not pay attention to what has been said, namely that the demonstrative syllogisms are necessary, / that the dialectical ones are possible in the majority of cases,[4] that the rhetorical ones are possible in equal cases,[5] that they involve neither inclination nor rarity,[6] and that the poetical ones are false and impossible. This is not the [proper] consideration; nor did the father of logic[7] indicate it.

As for sophistical syllogisms, they employ a proposition resembling others to which an experiential critical one is joined for the purpose of
464    producing error. / If the resemblance is to necessary propositions and the manner of their usage, the syllogizer is called "a sophist"; and if it is to widely-known propositions, the syllogizer is called "an agitator" and "a disputer." The agitator is the opposite of the dialectician, and the sophist is the opposite of the sage.[8]

---

[4] *Munkina akthariyya*. An example of this is the possibility of the growth of a beard for a man.

[5] *Munkina musāwiyya*, such as the possibility for middle-aged men to become bald.

[6] I.e., they are neither inclined in the direction of occurrence, nor away from it, toward rare occurrence. In other words, the chance of their occurrence is fifty-fifty.

[7] I.e., Aristotle.

[8] In this chapter Ibn Sīnā seeks to distinguish a demonstrative argument from other types of arguments. Five types of arguments are mentioned:

1. A demonstrative argument is characterized as having a certain conclusion, and which seeks to produce assent.

2. A dialectical argument may or may not have a true conclusion; after all, truth is not of its concern. Rather, its main concern is to defeat the opponent. And this may be achieved by the mere fact that the propositions are generally acknowledged. Like demonstration, a dialectical argument seeks to produce assent, but the cause of the assent in both is different: in the former, it is the certain truth; in the latter, it is the generally acknowledged information.

3. A rhetorical argument resembles the previous two in that it seeks to produce assent. But it differs from them in that it makes no explicit claim, whether to what is generally acknowledged, or to anything else – it simply makes no assertion.

4. A poetical argument differs from the previous three in that it does not seek assent; yet it is received in the soul by virtue of its resemblance or truth.

5. A sophistical argument is one which seeks to produce assent, not by virtue of being true or generally acknowledged, but by virtue of resembling the true and the generally acknowledged.

Thus of these five types of arguments, only the first is scientific for it is the only one of whose truth we are assured. The second, third and fourth may be true, but they are not scientific, for science cannot rely on maybes, but only on certitude. Finally, the fifth is never true.

## Chapter Two. Remark: Concerning the syllogisms and the demonstrative inquiries

The scientific inquiries may be the result of the necessity of a judgment,[9] the possibility of a judgment, or the absolute existence, in a non-necessary sense,[10] / as is the knowledge of the states of the conjunction and opposition of the stars. Every genus [of these inquiries] has its proper premises and conclusion. Similarly, the demonstrator infers the necessary from the necessary, and the non-necessary from the non-necessary, be that mixed or pure.[11] / Therefore, do not pay heed to him who says that the demonstrator does not employ, except necessary propositions and those that are possible in the majority of cases, without others. Rather, if he wishes to infer the truth of a possible in a minority of cases,[12] he uses the possible in a minority of cases.[13] And in every type [of inquiry] appropriate [premises] are used. Nothing but this has been stated by earlier scholars,[14] but in a manner overlooked by recent ones. That is the earlier scholars said that in demonstration the necessary conclusion is inferred from necessary propositions, / and in other than demonstration it may be inferred from non-necessary propositions. Nothing was intended but this. Or what was intended is that the truth of the premises of the demonstration is, in their necessity, possibility or absoluteness, a necessary truth. When "necessary" is stated in the book *On Demonstration*,[15] what is intended by it is that which is common to the necessary, mentioned in the book / *On the Syllogism*,[16] and that whose necessity endures as long as the subject

---

[9] I.e., absolute or unconditioned necessity.

[10] I.e., unreal or conditioned necessity.

[11] I.e., whether the premises are a mixture of non-necessary and necessary propositions, or non-necessary propositions only, the conclusion is non-necessary.

[12] *Munkina aqalliyya*, such as the possibility for women to go bald.

[13] In other words, a demonstration is not necessarily one in which a thing is shown to have a 100% chance of occurring (necessary) or that it has somewhere between a 50% and a 99% chance of occurring (possible in the majority of cases), but also one in which a thing can be shown to have even a 1% chance of occurring (possible in a minority of cases).

[14] I.e., Aristotle.

[15] I.e., *Anal. Post.*

[16] I.e., *Anal Pr.*

## CHAPTER 2

remains qualified by that which qualifies it; and not the pure necessary.[17]

In the premises of the demonstration, essential predicates are used, under the two aspects [mentioned] earlier,[18] attributed to the "essential" in the premises. / But in the inquiries, the constitutive essentials are never sought.[19] You have already learned this, and learned the error of him who opposes it. Rather, [in them], the essentials are only sought in the other sense.

---

[17] I.e., the unconditioned or absolute necessary. In *Sh. Bur.* (p. 122), these two senses of necessity are described as follows: "If in the book *On the Syllogism*, we say that every C is by necessity B, we mean that whatever is described as C – in whatever manner it is so described: always, by necessity, for some time or by non-necessary existence – then it is described at all times and always as B – even if it is not described as C.

"While as, if we say in this book [(*On Demonstration*)] that every C is B by necessity, we mean that whatever is described by necessity as C is described as B. This is a more general notion than that [than the previous notion of necessity]; that is, whatever is described as C, as long as it is so described, is described as B – even if it is not such – as long as its essence exists."

[18] These are the two senses attributed to the "essential" in the First Method: the constitutive essential and the essential accident.

[19] The predicates of the premises of a demonstrative inquiry cannot be of the constitutive essential type. This is so because the constitutive essential is evident (*Naj.*, p. 71). But an inquiry is a search for evidence. The predicates in the inquiry can be essential accidents. On the other hand, in the demonstration itself they can be essential in both senses indicated above. However, they cannot be of the constitutive essential type in both premises. The reason is this. If the major term is a constitutive essential of the middle one, which in turn is constitutive of the minor term, then the major is a constitutive essential of the minor (by the principle "the constitutive of a constitutive is constitutive"). But this is impossible, except in two cases:

(1) When the subject is known only by external things, or just by the name; that is, when the essence is still unknown. This is exemplified in the question, "Is the soul a substance or not?" One who asks this question must know the name for the soul but not its essence.

(2) When, by demonstration, one does not seek both the fact and the cause – in the Fifth Chapter of the present method, a demonstration seeking the former will be called "factual demonstration," and a demonstration seeking the latter "causal demonstration" – but the cause alone. An example of this is when, after knowing that the human being is a substance which is not a primary principle (by "primary" here is meant that which is stated of the subject universally, but not of anything more general or more particular than it), we wish to demonstrate the cause, and so we say, "... because he is a body" (ibid.).

474 Chapter Three. Remark: Concerning the subjects, principles, questions [and transference of demonstrations][20] in the sciences

For every one of the sciences, there is one or more things appropriate
475 to it and whose state or states we investigate. These states are / the essential accidents, and the thing is called "the subject" of that science such as proportions for geometry.

Further, for every science there are principles[21] and questions. The principles are the definitions and the premises of which the syllogisms of the science are composed. The premises are either [1] propositions that must be accepted, [2] propositions that are admitted by virtue of confidence in the teacher – these are given in the preface to the
476 science, / or [3] propositions that are admitted for the time being, and until they are made evident, concerning these there is doubt in the student's soul.

As for the definitions, they are like the definitions which are given of the subject of a discipline, of its parts and of its particulars, if it has any,[22] and like the definition of its essential accidents. These too are given in the preface to the sciences.

The propositions that are admitted by virtue of confidence in the
477 teacher / and the definitions may be grouped under the name "assumption," [23] and thus they are called "assumptions." Of these the admitted propositions are properly called "posited principles." [24] And "postulates" [25] is the name given to admitted propositions under the

---

[20] Even though the transference of demonstrations in the sciences is not mentioned in the title of the present chapter and is mentioned in the title of the next one, we have chosen to include it in the former and exclude it from the latter. This is because while the last statement of the present chapter refers to it, there is no mention of it at all in the next chapter.

[21] The subject, principles and questions are the three necessary elements in a science. All three must be known prior to demonstration.

Principles are divided into (1) definitions and (2) premises, which in turn divide into (2.1) propositions that must be accepted; (2.2) propositions admitted by virtue of confidence in the teacher, and (2.3) propositions admitted with doubt in the student's soul. (1) and (2.2) are subsumed under the name "assumptions," (2.2) under the name "posited principles," (2.3) "postulates," and (2.1) "disciplines."

[22] Text: *in kānat* (if they are).

[23] *Al-waḍ'*.

[24] *Al-aṣl al-mawḍū'*.

[25] *Muṣādarāt*.

second aspect.[26] If a certain science has posited principles, these must be presented at the beginning, as an introduction to the science.

As for the propositions that must be accepted, there is no need for enumerating them.[27] But [the name] "disciplines"[28] may be reserved for them. These must be presented at the beginning of the totality of the premises. Thus the demonstration for any posited principle in a science is drawn from another science.

479 *Chapter Four. Remark: Concerning the correspondence of the sciences*[29]

You must know that if the subject of a certain science is more general than that of another science, [it is such] either

[1] under the aspect of determination,[30] that is, [A] by having one of them, the more general, as a genus for the other; [B] by having the subject in one of them, [in] the more general, taken in an absolute 480 sense, and in the other as restricted by a peculiar state. / It is customary to call the more particular, a subject subordinate to the more general. An example of the former is the science of solids under geometry. And an example of the latter is the science of movable spheres under the science of spheres. And both aspects[31] may be united in one whose more appropriate name is "subordinate subject." An example of this is the science of perspectives under the science of geometry. /

481 [2] The subject of a certain science may be different from that of another science, but it is considered inasmuch as it has appropriate[32]

---

[26] According to Aristotle, type (1) of these premises has been demonstrated. And types (2) and (3) are not yet demonstrated but are demonstrable. "Hypothesis" is the name he gives to type (2); and "illegitimate postulate" is the name he gives to type (3) (*Anal. Post.*, I, 10).

[27] For they have already been enumerated in the Sixth Method.

[28] *Al-sinā'a*.

[29] Text: concerning the transference of demonstrations and the correspondence of the sciences. See note 20 for deleting "transference of demonstrations."

[30] I.e., in terms of the essence.

[31] I.e., A and B.

[32] Text: *khāṣṣa*. We have avoided translating this as "proper" or "peculiar" since what is said to pertain to the subject of a science cannot be said to be proper or peculiar to another.

accidents that pertain to the subject of that science. And thus it is also a subject subordinate to that science. This is exemplified in music under the science of arithmetic. /

482 Most of the posited principles in a particular science which is made subordinate to another are nothing but true in the universal science which is made superior [to it]. For often the principles of the superior universal science are true in the subordinate particular one. /
483 A science may be superior to one science, and subordinate to another. This leads to the science whose subject is the Existent inasmuch as It exists, and which investigates Its essential attributes. This is the science called "first philosophy."

485 *Chapter Five. Remark: Concerning causal demonstration and factual demonstration*[33]

If the middle term is the cause in the thing itself[34] for the existence of the judgment which is the relation of the parts of the conclusion to each other, then the demonstration is a causal demonstration, since it gives the cause of assenting to the judgment, and the cause of the existence of the judgment. Thus it gives the cause with no restriction. /

486 If the middle term is not such, but is the cause of the assent only — thus giving the reason for the assent without giving the reason for the existence [of the judgment] — then the demonstration is called "factual demonstration," since it indicates the factuality of the judgment in itself, without its cause in itself.

If, in the factual demonstration, the middle term, in addition to not being a cause of the relation of the two terms of the conclusion, is an

---

[33] *Burhān lima wa-burhān inna.* In the former, the middle term is the cause of the relation of the two terms of the conclusion, both in the mind and in external reality. This type of demonstration does not only tell us that a thing is but also why it is; hence the name "*lima*" (reason, or cause). In the latter, on the other hand, the middle term is the cause of the relation of the two terms of the conclusion, but only in the mind. This type of demonstration gives us no information about the cause of the thing in external reality, but only that it is. Hence the name "*inna*" (that it is, or the fact). This distinction between causal demonstration and factual demonstration is analogous to the distinction drawn by Aristotle between knowledge of the reasoned fact and knowledge of the fact (*Anal. Post.*, I, 13).

[34] I.e., in external reality.

effect of the relation of these two terms and is better known to us [than it], then it is called "indicative." [35] / An example of this is your saying, "If there is a lunar eclipse, then the earth is in an interposition between the sun and the moon; but there is a lunar eclipse, therefore, the earth is in an interposition." [36] You must know that the repeated part functions as a middle term. The interposition was made evident by the eclipse which is the effect of the interposition. Whereas in the causal demonstration, the case is contrariwise; thus the eclipse is made evident by the evidence of the interposition of the earth.

It is possible for you to construct a predicative syllogism of either type [of demonstration] with common terms. Let the minor term be "fever-ridden" and the other two terms "a pricking, penetrating shudder" and "tertian fever" – of the two, the effect being the shudder. /

You must know that it is not the same thing to say, "The middle term is a cause for the existence of the major term, without restriction, or it is its effect, without restriction," as it is to say, "It is a cause or an effect of the existence of the major term in the minor one." This is among what has been overlooked. Rather, you must know that often the middle term is an effect of the major term, but a cause of the existence of the major in the minor.

*Chapter Six. Remark: Concerning the questions [in the sciences]*

Of the principal questions, there are

[1] the question, "Is the thing, absolutely?" or "Is it in such and such a state?" He who asks this question asks about one of the two contradictory extremes.

---

[35] *Dalīlan*. This term is used by Ibn Sīnā to refer to both the middle term in a factual demonstration, which is not only not the cause of the relation of the two terms of the conclusion, but is the effect of this relation, as well as to the demonstration itself which includes such a middle term. Every indicative demonstration is a factual one, but the reverse is not true.

[36] This is a repetitive syllogism in which what functions as a middle term, "there is a lunar eclipse," is not only not the cause of the relation of "the earth" to "an interposition between the sun and the moon," which is the conclusion, but it is caused by this relation. If the earth is interposed between the sun and the moon, then a lunar eclipse occurs.

[2] The question, "What is / the thing?" By this question, one may ask about what the quiddity of the thing is, or about what the comprehension of the name used is. The question, "What is the thing?" must precede the question, "Is it?" if what is indicated by the used name, regardless of the manner of its existence,[37] is not a comprehended term in the question – an explication of the name in the question is then sought. / If existence is verified for the thing, that itself becomes a definition of its essence, or a description, if it is permissible for it [to have a definition or a description].[38]

[3] The question, "Which thing is it?" This question is also considered among the principal questions. By this question, one seeks to distinguish the thing from other things. And

[4] The question, "What is the reason for the thing?" [In this question] it is as if one asks about what the middle term is, if the purpose is to obtain assent only, by the answer to the question, "Is it?" or about what the cause is, if the purpose is not the assent by that only – and in whatever manner – but the search for the cause in the thing itself.[39] / There is no doubt that this question is posterior in order to the question, "Is it?" whether in potentiality, or in actuality.[40]

Among the questions, there are also

[5] "How is the thing?"
[6] "Where is the thing?" and
[7] "When is the thing?"

These are particular questions that are not among the principal ones. Rather, one declines to consider them among the principal questions. Often they are dispensed with by using instead the question, "Is it?" – in the compound form[41] – / if these "how," "where," and "when" are discerned, yet without knowledge of their relation to the subject whose state is in question. But if these are not discerned, then the question, "Is the thing?" cannot replace these

---

[37] *Wa-kayfa kān.*
[38] I.e., if the thing is not simple.
[39] I.e., in external existence.
[40] It is only after you know whether a thing exists or not that it makes sense to ask, "Why does it exist?" or "Why does it not?"
[41] An example of the question, "Is the thing?" in the compound form is "Is George at school?" This is to be contrasted with the question, "Is the thing?" in a simple form, which is exemplified by "Does George exist?"

questions.[42] And thus these become questions which lie outside what have been considered [as principal questions].

---

[42] Put simply: if you need to inquire about the relation of something specific to the subject that you have in mind – be that a state, a place or a time, you can employ the question, "Is the thing?" instead of "How is the thing?" "Where is the thing?" or "When is the thing?" If, on the other hand, there is no specific state, place or time whose relation to the subject you need to inquire about, then the above-mentioned substitution cannot be performed. For example, if you wish to know whether George is pale, you can ask, "Is George pale?" while if there is no such specific quality that you wish to know if George possesses, but you wish to inquire about his state in general, it would be more appropriate to say, "How is George?"

# The Tenth Method

## ON FALLACIOUS SYLLOGISMS

Error may occur either [1] because of the syllogism. That is [A] when what is claimed to be a syllogism is not one in its form – when it is not under the form of a figure which yields a conclusion; [B] when it is a syllogism in its form, but it yields a conclusion other than the one sought; / [C] when what is not a cause had been posited in it as a cause; or [D] when it is not a syllogism with respect to its matter. That is, it is such that if the necessary in its matter is taken into consideration, its form is then corrupted. And if what it involves, in the previously-mentioned manner, is admitted, it is a syllogism, but one which must not be admitted. Thus if one considers the ambiguity of the states of the middle term in the two premises, and the states of the two extremes in them, and the conclusion, then its admission is not necessary. Hence even though it is a syllogism in its form, still it must not be accepted. You have already learned the difference between the two. [The syllogism in which] what is not a cause is posited as a cause is of this sort.[1] And [E] begging the question[2] / is also of this sort.[3] This [error] occurs when two of the terms of the syllogism are two names with one meaning, while they must have different meanings.

Thus if in the syllogism attention is paid to its form, and then to the state of its matter which we have indicated, no error occurs, because of ignorance / of the composition, to positing what is not a cause as a

---

[1] I.e., the sort of error that is due to the syllogism.
[2] Text: *al-muṣādara 'alā al-maṭlūb al-awwal* (postulating the first object of research at the beginning), i.e., in the premises – the first object of research being the conclusion. In this error, the conclusion is postulated at the beginning in direct demonstration; but in demonstration by contradiction, it is the contradictory of the conclusion that is given in the premises (*Naj.*, p. 93).
[3] I.e., the sort of error that is due to the syllogism.

499 cause or to begging the question. / That is it[4] [for the error that is due to the syllogism]. Or

[2] Error may occur in a syllogism which must be admitted but it is due to a cause in the premises, taken one by one.

[2.A] Error may occur because of equivocation in the comprehension of the expressions,[5] whether simple, composite – as you know – or a combination of both.

[2.A.a] An example of this is the error that may occur because of passing from the expression "all" to the expression "everyone," and vice versa, thus making what belongs to "everyone" belong to "all,"
500 and what belongs to "all" belong to "everyone." / But no doubt there is a difference between all and every one of the parts.

[2.A.b] But the passage may be by way of the division of the expression, such that if the expression is true when united, it is, then, believed that it is also true when divided. An example of this is believing that, if it is true to say, "Imru' al-Qays is a unique poet,"
501 then it is also true to say, / "Imru' al-Qays is unique," and "Imru' al-Qays, the dead, is a unique poet." Thus the dead is judged to be a poet. Again if it is true that "five" is even and odd, as united,[6] then it is true that "five" is even and that it is odd. /

502 [2.A.c] The passage may be the converse of this. That is, if it is true that "Imru' al-Qays is a poet," and that "He is good," then it is [assumed that it is] absolutely true that, in any manner you please, "He is a good poet," i.e., [good] at poetry. This too fits in with that in which, in some respect, error is caused by the meaning, but due to an equivocation in the expression. And thus these are fallacies that fit in with [those due to] the expression.

[2.B] Error may occur due purely to the meaning. This is exemplified in [the error] that occurs [a] because of imagining the converse; [b] because of taking what is by accident in place of what is
503 in essence; / [c] because of taking what follows the thing in place of

---

[4] Text: *hadhā* (this). This expression is sometimes used to mark the end of one part of a discourse and the moving on to another.

[5] The following examples show that in contrast to 1.E, where there is a community in the meaning of the expressions which is ignored, in the present case error consists of employing, in the premises of the syllogism, expressions that are thought to have the same meaning when they do not.

[6] In the sense that five is the union of two and three.

the thing; [d] because of taking what is in potentiality in place of what is in actuality; [e] because of overlooking what attaches to predication[7] that has been mentioned. / This you already know.

Thus you find that the causes of fallacies are limited to equivocation in expression, be that simple or composite in its substance; to the form and declension of the expression; and to the division of the composite and the composition of the divided. As regards [those] of meaning, [they are] imagining the converse; taking what is by accident in place of what is in essence; taking what follows the thing [in place of the thing]; overlooking what attaches to predication; positing as a cause what is not a cause; begging the question; and distorting the syllogism due to ignorance of its syllogistic character.[8] / If you wish, you may include in the fallacies of expression, the ambiguity of declension and being indeclinable, and that of diacritical marking.[9]

He who pays attention to the meaning and abandons what is suggested by the expression then considers, in the parts of the syllogism, meanings and not expressions, paying attention to them as they lead to their consequences; and does not violate in them what must be repeated in the two premises, nor in what must be repeated in the two premises and the conclusion; and further, takes into consideration the figure of the syllogism; and knows the types of propositions that we have enumerated; and after that presents this to himself in the manner that he who calculates would present what he imposes on himself – repeating and reviewing – and then makes an error, / deserves to abandon wisdom and the learning of it. Everyone is directed with facility toward that for which one was created.

I ask God, the exalted, for preservation and guidance. Praise to God who is our hope and the best of protectors!

---

[7] Such as the mode, the quantifier, etc.

[8] Notice that in this summary form and declension are said, for the first time, to be one of the sources of the fallacies that are due to the expression; and that taking what is in potentiality in place of what is in actuality is not listed as one of the sources of the fallacies that are due to the meaning.

[9] *Wa-shtibāh ash-shakl wal-i'jām.*

# Bibliography

al-Fārābī. *Al-Fārābī's Short Commentary on Aristotle's Prior Analytics.* Trans. Nicolas Rescher. Pittsburgh: University of Pittsburgh Press, 1963.
———. "Al-Fārābī's *Isagoge*," ed. D. M. Dunlop. *Islamic Quarterly*, 3 (1956), 117-138.
al-Ghazālī. *The Incoherence of Philosophers.* Trans. Sabīh Ahmad Kamali. Lahore: Pakistan Philosophical Congress, 1963.
Gohlman, William E. *The Life of Ibn Sīnā.* Albany: SUNY Press, 1974.
Gyekye, Kwame. "The Term *Istithnā'* in Arabic Logic." *Journal of the American Oriental Society*, 92 (1972), 88-92.
Ibn Rushd. *The Incoherence of Incoherence.* Trans. Simon van den Bergh. London: Luzac, 1954.
Ibn Sīnā. *Avicenna's Treatise on Logic.* Trans. F. Zabeeh. The Hague: Martinus Nijhoff, 1971.
———. *al-Ishārāt wat-Tanbīhāt.* Ed. Sulaymān Dunyā. 2nd edition. Cairo: Dar al-Ma'ārif fī Masr, 1971.
———. *al-Ishārāt wat-Tanbīhāt.* Ed. Jacques Forget. Leiden, 1892.
———. *al-Ishārāt wat-Tanbīhāt.* Ed. Nabil Shehaby. Tehran, 1960.
———. *Livre des directives et remarques.* Trans. A. M. Goichon. Paris: Librairie Philosophique J. Vrin, 1948.
———. *Mantiq al-Mashriqiyyīn.* Cairo: Salafiyya Press, AH 1328.
———. *an-Najāt.* Ed. M. S. al-Kurdī. Cairo, 1938.
———. *The Propositional Logic of Avicenna.* Trans. Nabil Shehaby. Dordrecht, Boston: Reidel, 1973.
———. *ash-Shifā', al-Ilāhiyyāt.* Ed. George Anawātī, Sulaymān Dunyā and S. Zāyed; revised and introduced by I. Madkour. Cairo, 1960.
———. *ash-Shifā', al-Mantiq, al-Burhān.* Ed. A. E. Afifi; revised by Ibrahim Madkour. Cairo, 1956.
———. *ash-Shifā', al-Mantiq, al-Madkhal.* Ed. I. Madkour, G. Anawātī, M. al-Khudairī and F. al-Ahwānī. Cairo: al-Matba'a al-Amīriyya, 1952.
———. *ash-Shifā', al-Mantiq, al-Qiyās.* Ed. S. Zāyed. Cairo, 1964.

Inati, Shams C. "An Examination of Ibn Sīnā's Solution for the Problem of Evil." Ph.D. dissertation; SUNY at Buffalo, 1979.
Madkour, Ibrahim. *L'Organon d'Aristote dans le monde arabe*. Paris: Vrin, 1934.
Porphyry. *Isagoge*. Ed. and trans. Edward W. Warren. Toronto: Pontifical Institute of Mediaeval Studies, 1975.
ar-Rāzī, Fakhr ad-Dīn. *Lubāb al-Ishārāt*. Cairo, AH 1355.
Rescher, Nicolas. *Studies in the History of Arabic Logic*. Pittsburg: University of Pittsburgh Press, 1963.
aṭ-Ṭūsī, Naṣīr ad-Dīn. *Commentary*. In Ibn Sīnā, *al-Ishārāt wat-Tanbīhāt*, ed. Sulayman Dunyā. Cairo, 1971.
Wolfson, Harry. "The Terms of *Taṣawwur* and *Taṣdīq* in Arabic Philosophy and Their Greek, Latin, and Hebrew Equivalents." *The Moslem World*, 33 (1943), 114-128.

# Index

absolute necessity 91-92, 93
absolute propositions 25, 91, 93-95, 109-112
absoluteness 102-103
accident of individual 15
accident, universal 15-16
accidental 17, 18, 5
admission 128
affirmation of propositions 78-79
al-Fārābī 131n.15, 72n.30, 129n.2, 131n.15
analogy 34-35, 49n.11, 129-130
Aquinas, St. Thomas 2
Aristotle 2, 22, 24, 35, 150-151, 154n.33; on accident 56n.32; on definition 70n.26; on finitude 65n.7; on first principles 119n.5; on knowledge 49n.7; on quick wit 121n.13; on syllogism 131n.3, 134n.23; on term 130n.10; on universal 53n.19
ar-Rāzī 4n.16
assent 5-6, 41, 42, 47, 49, 148-149; propositions involving assent 28-34, 118-128
aṭ-Ṭūsī 4n.16, 51n.14, 54n.27, 91n.6
Avicenna 24; see also Ibn Sīnā

beliefs 29-30, 119-125

certainty 38-40
common accident 18-19, 57, 67-69
complete expression 14, 51-52
complete induction 35
complete phrase 51-52
composite expression 14-15, 49n.9, 51
concomitant accidental 17, 54, 55-57, 62-63

concept 12, 48, 50-51; composite 6; simple 5-6; single 6, 8n.31, 48
conception 5-6, 12n.43, 41, 47, 49
concrete propositions 25, 94-95
conditional necessity 25, 92-93
conditional proposition 23-24, 36-38, 77-78, 83, 86-89; connective 23, 36, 37, 78, 86-87; disjunctive 23, 36, 37-38, 78, 87-88; real disjunctive 23, 38, 87-88; unreal disjunctive 23, 38, 87-88
constitutive essential 54-55
contradiction 26-27, 107-113; absolute propositions and 109-112; concrete propositions and 109-112; matters of propositions and 108-109; modes of propositions and 109-113
conversion 27-28; absolute propositions and 113-115; necessary propositions and 115-116; possible propositions and 116-117

definiteness 80-81, 82, 88-89
definition 19-21, 40-41, 49, 70-72; errors in 73-76
demonstration 38-43, 150-154; causal 40, 154-155; factual 40, 154-155; principles on which d. based 40-41; questions in 41-42, 155-157; subject of 41
demonstrative induction 35
description 19-21, 49, 72-73; errors in 73-76
difference 17-18, 19-20, 41, 65-66, 69; and definition 71-72

equipollence 83-86
essence 8, 10, 19-20, 40, 41n.90

essential 16-17, 53-55, 57-60
essential accident 57-58, 62-63
eternal necessity 25, 92; see also absolute necessity
explanatory phrase 8-9, 11, 19-21, 49-50
expression 48, 50-53

falsification 5n.21
figure 36-37; first 135-137; second 137-141; third 141-143

genus 17-18, 19-20, 58n.41, 59-60, 64-66, 69

Ibn Sīnā 1-4; on accidental 57n.37; on arguments 149n.8; on assent 5n.21; on certainty 39; on common accident 68n.21; on conditionals 78n.7; on description 20-21; on essential 16; on estimative propositions 124n.24; on expressions 12-13, 15; on knowledge 7-8; on logic 9-11; on modes of propositions 91n.6; on possibility 95n.18; on propositions 22-23, 23-24, 29-34, 39-40, 130n.9; on quiddity 55nn.29-30; on syllogism 131n.12, 131n.15; on time 52n.15
impossibility 25-26, 90n.1; see also necessity; possibility
incomplete expression 14
incomplete induction 35
incomplete phrase 52
indefinite propositions 80-82
individual expression 15, 52-53
induction 34, 35, 49, 129

knowledge 6-9

logic 9, 47-48; as branch of philosophy 9-11; function and use of 6-9

matters of propositions 24-25, 90-91
modes of propositions 25-26, 90n.1, 91-106; and particular propositions 103-104; absoluteness in 102-103; principles of 97-98; universal affirmative in 99-100; universal negative in 101-102

nature 8, 10, 40n.90, 81n.15
necessary concomitants 16
necessary proposition 93
necessity 25-26, 79n.11, 90n.1, 92-95, 103-106
negation of propositions 78-79
non-modal absolutes 25
non-modal propositions 91n.5
non-necessary absolute propositions 93-94

objects of assent 6-7
objects of conception 6-7

particular propositions 103-104
Porphyry 18, 68n.21, 76n.41
positiveness 83-86
posited principles 34, 152
possibility 25-26, 90n.1, 95-98, 103-106
postulates 34, 152-153
predicables 16-19, 64-69
predicate 51, 53-54
predicative proposition 22-23, 36-37, 77, 83, 88-89
premise 130-131
principles of syllogisms 32-34
proof 8-9, 11, 34-38, 49-50, 129-143
property 18-19, 67-69, 70
property, unreal 18
propositions 21-34, 76-89, 118-128; absolute 25, 91n.5, 93-95; admitted 29-30, 118, 119-125, 130; ambiguous 30, 119, 126-127; based on outside sources 30, 119, 125; based on unanimous traditions 28, 29, 119, 121; concrete 25, 95; containing syllogisms 29, 119, 121; determined 125, 148; estimative 28, 30, 119, 123-124; experiential 28, 29, 119, 120; imagined 28, 30, 119, 127-128,

# INDEX

148; intuited 29, 119, 121; non-modal 91n.5; non-necessary 25, 93-95; observational 29, 119, 120; presumed 28, 30, 118-119, 125, 126, 148; primary 29, 119-120, 128n.35; received 28, 125, 126, 148; reflective 120; sensible 28, 120; singular 80; widespread 28, 30, 119, 122-123, 128n.35, 148

quiddity 8, 40n.90, 54-55, 56n.33, 57-63, 70-71, 81n.15

reality 54-55
real property 18-19, 67n.16
relation of propositions 89
Rescher, Nicolas 24, 131n.15

sciences 152-154
separable accident 17, 19, 54, 57, 57n.36
single elements 48
single expression 13-15, 48n.5, 51
singular proposition 80
species 17-18, 19-20, 60n.49, 61n.50, 62n.55, 64-66, 70

statement, absolute 25
statement, non-modal 25
substance 58, 68, 69n.23
syllogism by contradiction 147; of equals 145
syllogisms 34, 35-38, 49, 130-135, 144-147; conditional conjunctive 144-145; conjunctive 35-37, 131, 132, 133; demonstrative 148; dialectical 148; fallacious 158-160; poetical 148; predicative 36-37; predicative conjunctive 134-143 (see also figure); repetitive 35, 37-38, 131, 132; repetitive conditional 145-147; rhetorical 148; sophistical 149; validity of 37-38, 42

universal accident 15-16
universal expression 15, 16-19, 52-53
universal language 48
universal propositions 101-102
universals 64-70; see also predicables
unreal property 18

GENERAL THEOLOGICAL SEMINARY
NEW YORK